An Instructional Guide to

AMATEUR

WRESTLING

D1564488

An Instructional Guide to

AMATEUR

WRESTLING

RUSS HELLICKSON

With ANDREW BAGGOT

A Perigee Book

Readers should be advised that wrestling, like any sport, can lead to injury. Every care and precaution has been taken in the preparation of this book to stress the need for safety consciousness and the importance of proper techniques. Always consult your doctor before beginning a training program, and be sure to stretch out and warm up before each practice. Responsibility for personal injury or property damage suffered while training or competing is expressly disclaimed, and rests solely with the reader.

Perigee Books
are published by
The Putnam Publishing Group
200 Madison Avenue
New York, NY 10016

All photographs courtesy Richard H. Strauss.

Library of Congress Cataloging-in-Publication Data

Hellickson, Russ.
An instructional guide to amateur wrestling.

1. Wrestling. I. Baggot, Andrew. II. Title.
GV1195.H45   1987   796.8'12   86-30511
ISBN 0-399-51269-1

Book design by The Sarabande Press
Typeset by Fisher Composition, Inc.

Printed in the United States of America
2   3   4   5   6   7   8   9   10

CONTENTS

Chapter 1

A LECTURE
and a LESSON

We've all heard lectures before. Somewhere along the line your mother, father, teacher, friend, or wife has bent your ear with the intention of improving your current state of mind. Call this a lecture if you want, but it's really more than that. It's a lesson plan to help you do things you never thought possible, an important plan that will help you now, and help you even more years down the road.

You'll hear about sacrifice. About dedication. About commitment. About achievement.

About becoming the best you can be.

And when you're finished, you may have a better understanding of yourself.

In the fall of 1971 I had an opportunity to compete on my second international team, the world championship team competing in Sofia, Bulgaria. I had an opportunity on that trip to room with a young man who is my idol in sports participation. His name is Dan Gable.

On one particular evening of that trip Dan Gable won the world championship. He was crowned number one in his weight class, 149.5 pounds, in the entire world. He impressed me that night, but what impressed me more was what happened the following morning.

When I got up Dan was not in the room. I didn't know where he was. I asked around a little bit and one of the coaches said he thought he was out running. Sure enough, forty-five minutes later, Dan Gable came back into the room. Clad in a sweatsuit, he sat down on the end of his bed and counted as the drops of sweat fell to the ground. I sat and I marveled at this man. The morning after he had won the gold medal as the best there is he was running. He was training for the next competition.

Almost a year to the day after I sat on my bed and watched Dan Gable silently counting drops as a pool of sweat grew beneath him, he became an Olympic champion. And he did so in a way that few in Olympic history ever have. He won the Olympic gold medal without having one single technical point scored against him. That is how much he dominated his competition.

Every time Dan Gable had an opportunity to prepare himself to be a little bit better than someone else, he took advantage of it. When someone else would have been sitting around after winning a world championship, he was running. He wanted to earn everything he accomplished in his life. And he felt that to deserve success, you had to work harder than anybody else.

Too many people demand of life rather than demanding of themselves. We live in a great society, and it's very easy to expect things to come our way. There's no country in the world like America. But sometimes we take a lot of it for granted. We do not challenge ourselves. We do not expect enough of ourselves.

When I was an assistant coach at the University of Wisconsin we had a young man by the name of Jim Haines, who came from Arcadia, Wisconsin, and had won a state title at 105 pounds in high school. Jim Haines decided he wanted to go to the University of Wisconsin and get a degree. He wanted to come and wrestle.

I remember Jimmy Haines during his first year because he was unable to score a point against anybody in our wrestling room. I can see him sitting on the bench, the tears rolling down his cheeks. Not complaining, though. Not whining. Just depressed because he wasn't quite good enough to do the job.

But he did not quit. He worked out two and three times a day. There were many weeknights and weekends Jim would ask me to stay and drill with him. Imagine that, working out with someone who outweighed you by more than a hundred pounds.

In 1976 Jim made the Olympic team that competed in Montreal with me, wrestling at 114.5 pounds. The following year, Jim's senior year at Wisconsin, he won an NCAA title. Jim was best at takedowns. During his senior season Jim recorded 224 takedowns in 39 matches, a school record that still stands. In the NCAA championships that year, Jim trailed his semifinal opponent, Johnnie Jones of Iowa State, by two points with time running out. With fourteen seconds left, Jim scored a takedown to tie the score, then proceeded to let Jones go for a one-point escape. Then, with seven seconds left, Jim scored another takedown to win by a single point. Jim's confidence in his ability is a testimony to his dedication and persistence. He believed in himself and put forth the effort needed to achieve the goals he had set for himself.

Jim Jordan set goals, too. When he entered college at Wisconsin after winning four Ohio state titles, he sat down and wrote down all the things he wanted to accomplish. Big Ten championship. NCAA championship. They were all milestones on Jim Jordan's road to success.

In 1985 Jim won the Big Ten title at 134 pounds and added the NCAA title two weeks later. In 1986, knowing the challenges he would face in defense of those titles, Jim worked harder than ever before. He cut extra weight. He made some tremendous sacrifices. So when Jim Jordan won his second Big Ten crown and added his second straight NCAA title two weeks later, he celebrated the end of a long, demanding, rewarding journey. He cried.

To be successful requires a lot of hard work. Those who have achieved success will tell you that the goal had been set for a long time. They had dreamed of what they sought, but at the same time they had recognized and been willing to make the tremendous sacrifice necessary to fulfill the dream.

I sincerely believe that the examples set by Dan Gable, Jim Haines, Jim Jordan and others like them show that anything that is humanly, physically possible can be achieved if one desires it badly enough. The key is to learn to demand of yourself rather than demand of life.

If you really want to give meaning to your life, you must learn to ask great things of yourself. If you do this, you can find that meaning, and you can achieve success. You must learn to be an individual with strong goals and the fortitude to seriously strive to attain them.

All of us have the capability to improve ourselves, but many of us fall short when it comes to making the effort to improve. In most cases we're willing to settle for less because we don't quite know how to go about getting what we want.

What about you? You've picked up this book so you must be interested. Why in the world would you want to begin wrestling? Big money opportunities? Glamour? A chance to become recognized? If these are your motives you are pursuing the wrong sport.

Wrestling is one of the most demanding physical and mental undertakings in competitive athletics. Wrestling requires commitment and sacrifice.

Why, then, do you want to be a wrestler?

To find the answer you must look within yourself. Do you have the desire? Do you want to make the most of your God-given talents? Do you want to set goals that now seem impossible? Are you prepared to make a commitment to achieving those goals? You must answer yes to all these questions if you are going to achieve success as a wrestler. And if you find success through wrestling, chances are you'll find it in life, too.

Let's begin with some history.

In 1984 the United States stepped up to one of its highest plateaus of achievement in the sport of wrestling. Competing against some of the world's finest athletes, Americans asserted themselves as never before. In a sport dominated by European countries, the U.S. won seven out of a possible ten gold medals in the freestyle discipline and four medals—including the first two gold medals ever—in Greco-Roman. The television coverage of those games, in which I took part as a color commentator for ABC Sports, put names like Blatnik, Banach, Baumgartner, Schultz and Fraser on the lips of wrestling followers all over the world. It also gave me a unique perspective on the sport I have come to love.

Wrestling encompasses the most essential and most coveted of human traits. Survival. Respect. Honor. Discipline. It is a sport that remains steadfastly attached to its ancient roots. It is a rule of life that to improve, to continue to make strides toward the future, an institution must change through the years. Yet wrestling has endured and prospered despite its refusal to change.

The first traces of the sport date back to 3000 B.C. Even then it was highly developed. Scenes sculpted on the walls of the temple-tombs of Beni Hasan near the Nile River in Egypt show numerous wrestling matches depicting practically every hold and fall combination used today.

Wrestling holds a prominent place in Greek mythology as well as in the Bible, in both of which the descriptions of the sport emphasize manhood and personal bravery. Pindar and other Greek poets write of the mightiest of Greek gods wrestling for possession of the earth on the highest mountain peaks. The first Olympian Games, which according to tradition took place near the river Alpheus at Olympia in 776 B.C., featured wrestling matches. The Bible tells us that in ancient times a wrestling match was used as a method for settling disputes. Any man who wished to gain, attain or regain his self-esteem had to know its secrets.

Wrestling did not come into prominence in the United States until the beginning of the twentieth century. The first organized intercollegiate match was held in 1900 and pitted the University of Pennsylvania against Yale. In 1904 wrestling's first conference—the Eastern Intercollegiate Wrestling Conference—was formed.

Today there are a number of wrestling disciplines that emphasize varying skills and rules. High school and college wrestlers in the United States operate under a rigid rulebook. Their scope is limited mainly in the area of offensive technique. International freestyle has a liberal scoring system with a wider range provided for throws and scoring. The Greco-Roman discipline insists the wrestler attack only from the waist up. The style, practiced by the ancient Greeks and Romans, calls for frequent throws in order to score and at times can be breathtaking to watch. In scholastic and freestyle a wrestler may attack any part of his opponent's body. However, illegal and dangerous holds are disallowed at all levels.

While the essence of wrestling has remained the same over the centuries, it nevertheless has undergone a gradual facelift of sorts during the last twenty years. To pin your opponent, to hold his shoulders on the mat, is still the primary goal of any wrestler. But the sport as a whole has been somewhat modernized to make it more appealing to the spectator. Newer rules have put the emphasis on aggressive, offense-oriented wrestling rather than on stalling tactics and defensive abilities. But by appealing to the paying customer amateur wrestling is not putting itself on the same block with fellows like Hulk Hogan, Andre the Giant and the other comic-book characters who call themselves professional wrestlers. These are entertainers, and they perform for an audience that has relatively little interest in the kind of wrestling we're talking about.

What we're talking about is sport in its purest form, about making a commitment and following through on it, about setting goals and reaching out to achieve them, about becoming a better person in body, mind and spirit. About being the best.

Chapter 2

THE BUILDING
BLOCKS

As you read this book, keep in mind that what we tell you isn't etched in stone. That goes for everything—technique, training, and conditioning. Everyone is different. We're not going to cover everything, either. We're going to emphasize the basics to give you a foundation to build on.

Wrestling is a flexible beast. Some things that might work for you simply won't do for the next fellow. Throws come naturally to some and they feel most comfortable doing them. Others are takedown-oriented. Still others excel on the mat, working for turns. It's the same thing in preparation. Not everyone's focus is the same. Some need to emphasize weight-training. Others must concentrate more heavily on weight control. And while everyone needs to drill and refine technique, work in those areas differs, too.

What you're going to read here is simply one man's method of doing things, and some of the points I've picked up along the way. Some of them I learned through my own experiences. Others came from competitors, colleagues and coaches.

In any event, this method has paid dividends for me both as an athlete and as a coach. Using this method is like using building blocks: You begin with a foundation, making it strong and fortified, and slowly work your way up. As with the building of any important structure, there can be no shortcuts. Everything must be measured and calculated in exacting detail. You must have patience and use only the finest materials. Soon, the pieces will fit together to form the ideal move, the ideal workout, the ideal wrestler, the ideal athlete.

While I coached at Wisconsin, I had the opportunity to instruct some great college and international-style wrestlers. I believe a large part of their success had to do with their ability to embrace this approach and make it work for them. I have brought this plan to Ohio State, and believe its track record of success will continue.

I hope this book can give you the same sense of purpose.

The best way to illustrate this method is to give you three distinctly different examples of athletes who incorporated the building-block format and made it work for them.

Their names are Jim Haines, Andy Rein and Lee Kemp. All were National Collegiate Athletic Association champions. All were national freestyle champions. All were Olympic team members. However, each emphasized different areas of techniques. Haines was a takedown artist, Rein loved throws, while Kemp was a methodical, calculating technician who varied his attack to suit the moment. Each formulated a plan of growth, building from within. Through this process each found his strengths—the things he felt most comfortable with—and improved on them. Each became a champion.

Here's their checklist for success:

- First, make a commitment to excellence. There is no honor, pride or satisfaction in mediocrity.
- Dream, dream, dream.
- Establish realistic goals. They provide direction and a means for assessing progress.
- Be willing to pay the price. Work to develop, improve and perform. Comprehend and use all physical, psychological and technical skills to be the best you can be.
- Motivate and participate. Don't manipulate. Create a burning desire to accomplish the goals set before you. Communication is the key.
- Your actions should reflect your personality and your philosophy. Don't try to be someone or something you're not.
- Be morally, spiritually and ethically sound.

Winning is an attitude, not an occurrence. And the biggest thing is not winning, but the effort put forth to achieve your greatest potential.

To reach your potential in wrestling you must be able to leave yourself open to instruction. Never assume you know more than the next guy. I've learned a lot, and am still learning from high school coaches. Besides, you'll never learn all there is to know in wrestling. If you have an open mind you'll learn something every day in every practice from every opponent.

The successful teacher, coach or wrestler is always willing to add to his source of knowledge. There are things you may never use in competition, and there are things you won't be comfortable with. But by opening yourself up to those ideas, you are making another step toward understanding yourself and the sport.

This book is not written so that everyone reading it will become an Olympic champion. That is not possible. But for those who have the desire and the ability, it just might help you become the best wrestler you can be.

Chapter 3

LAYING the GROUNDWORK

"To want to fly is not enough. You also have to have wings."

(Raiport)

I first heard the above quotation cited in a lecture on sports psychology by Dr. William Morgan at the University of Wisconsin. It has great truth to it and is very applicable to wrestling. There are many components of success, and we could debate endlessly over whether the psychological, physiological or technical aspect is the most important in building the wrestling champion. I suggest these all are segments of the "wings" needed to complement a drive to succeed in wrestling.

The primary emphasis of this book is on the technical aspects of wrestling. You should not assume that this is the most important aspect, but it certainly is a good place to begin our "flight."

If we do something a certain way for a period of time, it becomes habit. This can be both good and bad. From Day One when you are learning or teaching wrestling technique you must remember you are building a foundation not only of attitude and spirit, but of method, too. The foundation of technique must be sound if it is to take you to the top.

All development and training in wrestling should prepare an individual to beat the best or to try to beat the best. I've always said that the test of technique is how it holds up against the top 20 percent. There certainly are no techniques that will succeed all the time against everyone, but I'm convinced that certain sound techniques have a higher percentage of success no matter the competition.

The longer I work in wrestling the more it seems there is to know. Every day is a learning experience in the sport. I enjoy being around successful wrestlers and coaches, picking up more knowledge and variety. Though it is easy to be humbled by what one does not know, I'm hopeful I can eliminate some problem areas for others by sharing what I call "percentage" techniques. That's why this book was written—to help delineate what those techniques are and how to teach them.

This is not a comprehensive book of technique and it does not include all maneuvers. Rather, it is a book that presents a concept, applies principles to enforce that concept, shows skills that apply those principles, and presents some wrestling maneuvers that use those skills. It is a book of wrestling fundamentals.

- Concept
- Principles
- Skills
- Technique

Wrestling techniques can be complicated even for the most experienced athlete or coach. We all have a tendency to try to teach or try to learn too fast. We get *fancy* before we get *good*. Turn it around. Get good at wrestling fundamentals first: These can be relied on no matter what the level of competition. Look at wrestling in a simpler form and give continuity to your learning.

We are going to take a simple concept and let it work for us. Actually we are going to let it determine how we will work to become better at wrestling.

CONCEPT: OUR GREATEST PHYSICAL POWER IS IN THE HIPS

The hips are the strongest part of the human body. The largest muscle groups are found here. It stands to reason that if we use this power often and effectively, we can insure our greatest success in working technique. Proper hip position means more power in execution of any techniques. Success or failure of various attacks—working for or against takedowns, escapes, reversals, control and pins—can be tied to how effectively we let this hip power work for us.

PRINCIPLES

These are not carved in stone. There are times when we can and will make exceptions to the application of these principles. However, the beginning wrestler can build a strong, reliable foundation initially if he avoids exceptions. As we said before, you can get fancy later. Get good at the basics first. Make proper hip position automatic: Make it a habit.

Remember, the following principles apply to all techniques used on the feet or on the mat:

- Keep your head and shoulders above your hips. Leaning forward or dropping your head can be the beginning of disaster.
- Keep your thighs, hips, stomach and buttocks off the mat. Contact with the mat should be made only with your feet, knees, hands and elbows. Anything else is lazy and can be costly.
- Keep your elbows as close to your sides as possible. The closer your elbows get to your head the weaker your arms become.
- Pressure into your opponent. Make him carry your weight as much as possible. Be careful. Post him by forcing him to plant his weight in a position that works to your advantage; don't push him. There is a great difference. Hang on him; don't lean against him. Let gravity be your ally.
- Change your angle and your altitude. Rotating pressure is called *torque* and it's a way of gaining leverage. A simultaneous change of level and direction is tough pressure to beat.

If emphasized enough, these principles really make sense and will enhance your hip power regardless of your mode of attack. Let them sink in. Really think about them and apply them to your wrestling. They will make a difference.

Now, let's apply these principles, using the hip power concept in the learning of fundamental skills. These skills represent basic body positions and common actions that, in varied combinations, will allow us to execute any wrestling maneuver.

Chapter 4

THE BASIC SKILLS

In the early 1970s, I served on the United States Wrestling Federation's instructional staff with six other coaches—Gray Simons, Ed Perry, Doug Blubaugh, J Robinson, Ron Finley and Terry McCann. Together we put together a list of Seven Basic Skills, which are still taught today. (The USWF is now USA Wrestling, the sport's governing body in this country. Written information and videotapes on the skills are still available through the USA Wrestling office at 405 W. Hall of Fame Ave., Stillwater, OK, 74075.)

The skills I present here include 10 distinct areas that will help you build that foundation for technical advancement. In some respects the skills are cumulative. The application of each allows you to better execute and understand skills you learn later.

1: STANCE

Body position is everything in wrestling. Our principles should make this skill very easy to grasp. The key is to maintain your stance throughout the wrestling match. When you lose your stance, you sacrifice effectiveness because of loss of power.

You must work on stance in every practice session. Be conscious of the three H's—head, hips and hands—as you work to maintain a correct stance.

Your head must be up and somewhat bulled. Look ahead, not down. Your hands should be in front of your body with your elbows kept in close proximity to your hips. Your hips, your center of gravity, should stay underneath your head and shoulders as much as possible. If you get your head and shoulders too far forward, you will fall forward when pressured. In this situation, your poor stance becomes a good set for your opponent.

Keep your knees bent and about shoulder-width apart. You can use either a staggered stance (in which one foot leads the other) or a square stance. You should be able to use both. Stay on or get to your feet as much as possible. Going to your knees is more desirable than going to your stomach or buttocks, but it still limits your mobility.

Square stance (left) and staggered stance (right)

Your down stance is important, too. Every rule that applies while you are on your feet applies here as well. Keeping your hips under you is vital. Stance and hip power are synonymous no matter where you are on the mat. *Keep your stance.*

I've spent a lot of time analyzing technique on videotape. It is a great learning tool. Watch a good match in slow-motion video. When someone attacks, or counters and scores, note the stance of the loser. After you have watched several matches, the importance of stance should become very clear to you.

Here are some observations worth making:

- Wrestlers do win with lousy stances. They are just better than their opponents.
- Wrestlers do lose with great stances. The other guys are just better. There are many factors involved in making a wrestler great.
- Wrestlers lose their stance when they get tired. It's not easy to maintain stance. It requires work and concentration. That's why you must use and emphasize it with all your technique.

Stance is the framework to which we will add our other skills and techniques. So whether you're going for a takedown, looking for an escape or reversal, in control or straining for the fall, your stance is critical to your success. Without it you can't use your full power.

2: MOTION

Wrestling is action and reaction. Sometimes we forget that and consequently do a lot of standing around.

The better wrestlers are movers. They constantly adjust and change their position. Motion creates momentum. Momentum creates additional pressure. Pressure creates a reaction. That's good wrestling.

There are two types of motion:

Foot and hip motion: You've got to move around on the mat. Movement can be forward and backward, but the most effective is lateral rotation. Move in a direction across and around your opponent. Cut him off. Never take long, high steps, and avoid crossing your feet. Keep your movements short and quick. Rotate your hips and pivot your feet.

Upper-body motion: This is the constant change of shoulder, arm, hand and head position. Of course, there are endless variations to how this motion can work. The experienced wrestler learns to move from position to position to help set up maneuvers as he gets his opponent to react.

Combining foot and hip motion and upper body motion well makes a good wrestler great. If you are going to have good, effective motion, you've got to be in good condition and always maintain your stance as you move.

3: *CHANGING LEVELS*

It is natural to lower your level by bending over. This results in the loss of power because the stance is poor. Learn to change levels by bending the knees and squatting (fig. 1) or by splitting the legs in a scissor step (fig. 2).

Changing levels by bending the knees

L (in the light singlet) executing a scissor step

The forward and rear legs move simultaneously in the scissor action. The key to changing levels is to let your hip weight settle over your legs.

You must be able to change levels as you move without losing your stance. You change levels by lowering or raising your hips, not your head and shoulders. Getting lower than your opponent in a power position is very important to successful wrestling.

4: PENETRATION

Penetration is simply creating pressure by driving your hips into and through your opponent. When you penetrate, your hips must follow a knee through the motion.

Because a lot of beginning wrestlers bend over to change levels, they drive with the head and shoulders and end up overextended on their penetration. Keep your stance as you penetrate.

Your penetration skills are not just for takedowns. They will help you succeed when pinning, reversing, escaping or riding. Driving your weight in and over your knee puts pressure into your opponent regardless of your mode of attack.

There are four variations of penetration, shown here from the takedown position.

1. **Angle knee drop:** This is penetration to the side that uses a rotation motion of the hips coming from the outside and driving to the inside. L (light jersey) comes from a square position with D (dark jersey, fig. 1) to the angle knee drop (fig. 2). L's right knee and hips are driven down and in toward D.

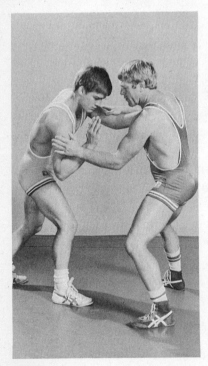 

Figure 1   *Figure 2*

2. **Knee over toe:**
   This is the standard penetration, straight in and under the opponent. After a scissor-step level change, wrestler D drives into L with knee-over-toe penetration. His knee will drive to the mat in a direction straight through L's legs.

3. **Inside knee drop, outside step:** The inside right knee of D drops toward the mat as the outside knee steps into L. This differs from the angle knee drop penetration in that the rotation of D's hips comes from the inside, driving to the outside of L, while still pushing to his right off his left foot.

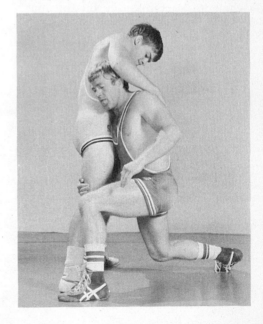

4. **Double knee drop:**
Both knees are
dropped in and under
together. This is ac-
complished by L by
pushing off the toes,
bending the knees and
letting gravity do its
work.

   Remember, keep your
stance, work your motion,
change your level and
penetrate into your
opponent.

5: LIFTING

At no time in wrestling is your opponent more vulnerable than
when he is completely off the mat within your grasp. The key to
lifting is learning to *lift* with
the hips and *squeeze* with the
arms. The tendency is to try to
pull up with the arms, which
puts more stress on an extended back and results in a
looser hold.

   Lifting from six different
positions is essential to totally
prepare a wrestler.

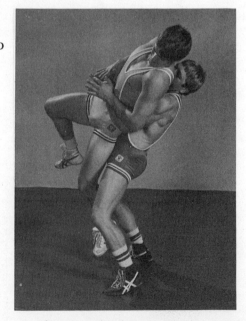

1. **Lift from behind:** D
keeps the arms low and
tight on the waist. He
walks the hips under in
a slight arch and pulls L
onto his hips.

2. **High double lift:** D's head is to the outside facing L's back and the left arm is across L's body, pulling down and in on the far hip. D's right arm is high on the leg under the buttocks, pulling tightly toward his waist.

3. **Head outside single leg:** D's head is outside the body as he controls L's near leg. His left hand is high in L's crotch and pulls L's buttocks tight. D's right hand locks behind L's knee, pulling down and into his waist.

   As you squat under to lift, step across your opponent's body with the front leg to add leverage to your lift.

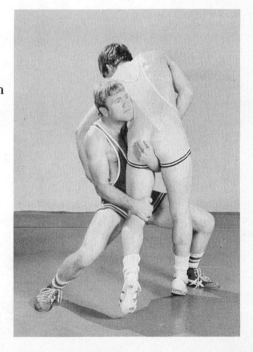

4. **Single lift, both hands on leg:** D squeezes the leg tightly and as high in the crotch as possible. D's head is now inside, facing L's stomach. Again D walks the hips under with a slight arch.

5. **Single lift, one hand on waist, one hand on leg:** D's left hand controls L's leg just above the knee and pulls it down and into D's waist. His right hand pulls down and in on L's hip. D steps slightly behind L with his right leg as he squats to lift.

6. **Body lock lift:** Both hands are locked around the body. D includes L's arm in his lock, but this is not essential to the maneuver. This lift should always be done from the side. Lock low on the waist and squat under and through the hips to lift.

Take particular note of the great head position for D on these lifts. If the head drops, the lifts are much more difficult. Move the feet by walking under as you lift. Let motion create momentum to help the lift.

6: ARCH AND TURN

Every wrestler should be able to arch and turn to the front of his shoulder. L assists D in learning the skill by holding his off arm for support.

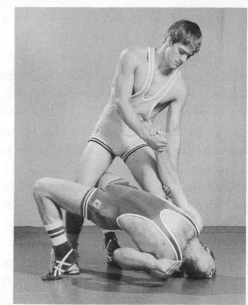

Two views of the arch-and-turn maneuver

Figure 1

Figure 2

Another method for teaching the arch and turn is shown in the photos above. L plants his left foot deep to the side of D (fig. 1) to support his weight. D punches his hips into L's right leg, walking his knee over his toes. Notice the position of D's hips under L. At this point (fig. 2) D pops his hips upward, carrying L's weight as he turns to the front of his left shoulder. L will end up on his back with D in pinning control above him.

Remember to keep the arms pulled tight as you arch. Many wrestlers fail with the arch and turn because they do not maintain hand control throughout the execution. If your body falls away because your hands release, you will lose effectiveness. Create pressure by pushing into your opponent or having him drive into you. This makes it easier to thrust your hips into and under him for power.

The photo above shows D executing an arch and turn from a single-leg lift position. Do not fall to your back or drop to your butt when performing this skill. Make sure you have adequate mat protection and knowledgeable supervision.

7: BACK STEP

Just as we can throw facing our opponent in the arch and turn, we can turn away from him and throw with the back step skill.

The hips still carry the weight. The photo at right shows how this footwork skill begins. L's right foot is planted toward D and his left foot steps behind it.

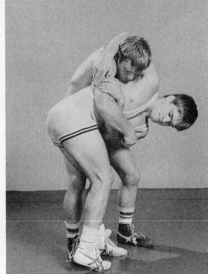

Arm throw   Figure 1   **Figure 2**

Headlock
throw
Figure 3

As he drives off his left leg and pivots on both feet, L's hips rotate across in front of D and to the side (figs. 1 and 2). L uses an arm throw and headlock combination to demonstrate this skill. The knees must bend and the hips drop and rotate to make this maneuver effective. Once the hips are through past D's body, L pushes off his feet to lift as he leans in the direction he will fall (fig. 3).

Hip sag

Here is a variation of the full back step, called the hip sag. Instead of stepping in with his right leg to initiate the back-step, D drops the right leg back, extends it and rotates the right hip down and into the mat. The quick and powerful change in level takes L out of position and ultimately to his back.

8: HIP LIFT

This is an easy skill to explain, but a difficult one to execute. It is often slighted, but it can play a big role in making you a complete wrestler.

In the photo above, L uses a hip lift with an arm underhook by turning his hip underneath D's body and elevates D's hips and left leg by lifting with his right leg. L pulls down and forward on D's upper body while pushing into D by driving off his left leg. L rotates his right hip into D while still lifting with his right leg. L will move in a rotating motion, hopping to his right and rear, maintaining this pressure until D collapses to the mat.

When you use this skill you may adjust back to other skills. You can go from this hip lift position on one foot to a backstep or an arch and turn depending on the opponent's reaction to the hip lift. You must move your feet and adjust your hip position by rotation to make these work.

In the photo above we see another situation in which the hip-lift skill is used. L controls D's right arm at the elbow and also controls L's left shoulder area with a lat (latissimus dorsi muscle) hook. L uses the hip lift to block D's right leg. L pulls down and to the right with his upper-body control and rotates his right hip into and across D. L hops off his left leg for balance and power. D will fall to his back at an angle forward and to the right.

Footsweep

9: FOOTSWEEP

A footsweep requires getting your opponent to lean into you as you step into him, and then rotating him over a posted foot. In the above photo, D is shown executing this skill.

Notice how close D's hips are to L. Wrestlers try to do this skill by keeping their hips back and reaching with the leg. It will not work. D has stepped into L with his right foot and posts or blocks with his left. The move will be completed with L falling to the mat on his right hip as he rotates over his posted right leg. D should not drive forward into L. Rather he steps in and rotates his hip under L because of L's pressure forward.

As I mentioned earlier, these skills are cumulative. I really think it is difficult to do a footsweep if the wrestler hasn't mastered to some degree the arch and turn. The same relationship exists between a back step and a hip lift. You must develop confidence in placing your hips into and under your opponent as opposed to always bending over and pulling them away. The skills tie together.

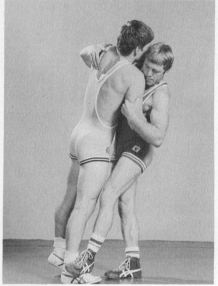

Figure 1   **Figure 2**

Here (fig. 1) D executes a footsweep from an over-under tie. In fig. 2, D also shows a footsweep from a head-outside lift position. Here D's left knee cuts L's leg out on the lift (fig. 2). The skill is still the same, however. D's slight arch position and right lead foot position are the same as in any other footsweep. You must step in with a lead leg and post with the other as you rotate.

This photo at right shows a continuation of the footsweep from the lift position. Notice how L is rotating to the mat in a direction toward and under D. Your upper-body action must bring your opponent in and around you in this fashion on any footsweep to make it effective. The skill does not change. To finish the footsweep here, D would need to penetrate to his left knee as he pulls L down to the mat on his back.

Footsweep

10: ELBOW POST–HIP HEIST

A hip heist is an explosive rotation of the hip that facilitates both a change in hip position and a change in hip direction. A series of photos show the use of elbow post–hip heist skill off a stand-up position.

L stands up and pushes back into D (fig. 1). L posts on his elbow to prevent falling to his hips or back on the mat (fig. 2). L twists his hips, bringing his right hip under and rotating his left hip back over

Figure 1

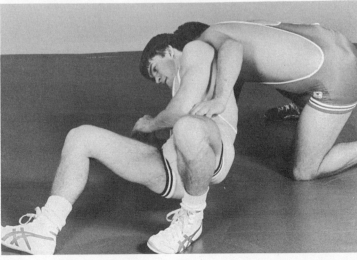

Figure 2

to force his stomach toward the mat (fig. 3). L's right leg scissors under and through his left leg as he rotates his hips to bring the left leg and knee back to the mat. L pushes back to a hip power position off his elbow to his hand to complete the hip heist (fig. 4).

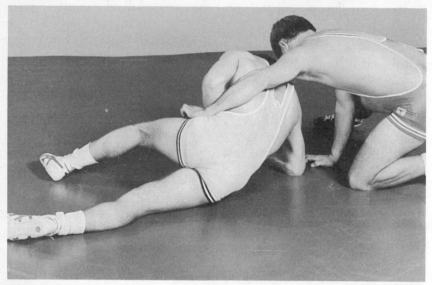

Figure 3

Figure 4

Again, this skill must be a quick and explosive rotation of the hips. Never allow your weight to settle on your hip into the mat. The twisting of the torso, while pushing off the planted elbow and simultaneously cutting the leg through, is what makes this skill effective.

It is possible to do this skill off a posted hand instead of the elbow.

The elbow post will bear more weight than the hand post, but wrestlers should be schooled in the use of both positions.

All of these skills will be applied in executing technique in the chapters ahead. They will have many applications, often in unexpected areas.

Wrestlers and coaches often choose to bypass teaching some of the skills, deciding they are not needed for their particular style of wrestling. This can be costly in the long run. By the same token, you can't learn these skills by using them once in a while. They have to be practiced and emphasized over and over again. You can't build if your foundation is shaky and weak. Make the basic skills second nature and they will make you a winner.

As we move into the technique area of this book, I want to emphasize and clarify a couple of points.

Wrestling is an action-reaction sport. You may like a maneuver and get very good at executing it, but that doesn't mean you will be able to use it on everyone. You need variety to succeed.

You must learn to let your opponent's position and pressure dictate your maneuvers. Remember, you are trying to use your greatest hip power, all the time, and take away your opponent's hip power—all the time.

Let your knowledge of principles and skills affect your wrestling. Practice them individually over and over again so you can use them reflexively. No method of executing a technique, maneuver or option in wrestling is always wrong or always right. I've seen some pretty bizarre ways of scoring points in wrestling. You've got to decide which ones are *dependable* and will *consistently* succeed. Those "percentage" techniques, as I call them, will take you the farthest.

The skill approach presented in this book and the hip power concept can start you down the right road in search of those winning techniques. The more exposure you can get to various techniques, the better you will become. Seek out the best. Get videotapes of the top wrestlers at all levels—high school, college and Olympic style. Watch them, study them and learn.

The more you wrestle the better you will become. Though this book is aimed at beginning wrestlers and our high school/collegiate rules, the principles, skills, and techniques taught can transcend any rules variation.

Don't isolate yourself in just one style. You only limit your potential.

I strongly encourage wrestlers and coaches to also pursue the international styles, both freestyle and Greco-Roman. These are used in both the World Championships and the Olympic Games. I think the different styles can complement one another. And who knows where your dreams, tied to your skills, might take you.

Chapter 5

TAKEDOWNS

An ability to complete a variety of takedowns is essential if you want to be a good wrestler. Nothing will have as dynamic an impact on your individual improvement as work in the takedown area. No matter what style of wrestling you compete in, takedowns can ultimately make you a winner.

Statistics have shown that the wrestler scoring the first takedown in a match wins more than three-fourths of the time. A takedown occurs when you move behind your opponent into a position of control. There are many ways to accomplish this. Let's look at some of them.

HIGH HEAD INSIDE SINGLE: LEG IN THE MIDDLE

L controls D's knee tight to his stomach. L's right hand, coming from the outside, locks over his left hand. L puts pressure on the leg by pulling it down and into his body. This downward pressure, as in all wrestling positions, makes D react. As he reacts, you can adjust your options to take him down.

L works to maintain his good stance all the time. Keep those elbows tight to the side and the head high. L should be able to move forward, backward, and in a rotating fashion with this leg in control. He must be able to keep good position first if he is ever going to make this leg attack position work for him.

L can apply more pressure by rotating his shoulders into D's thigh and stepping his right leg a little deeper behind D. This second position makes a whizzer (overhook) counter initiated by D on L's right arm more difficult. However, the whizzer does not stop the options if the attacker keeps a good stance. Changing off between these two leg control positions can make it harder for D to counter and easier to take him down.

DUMP (OPTION 1)

L rotates backward and to his left as he simultaneously changes levels and pulls D's leg in and down between his legs. L used this option because D drove into him and tried to straighten his left leg.

The pressure was right for this option to work. D. will fall to his buttocks as L continues to circle to his left. L must bend over a little to keep that right shoulder pressure on D's left thigh. However, most of the change in level comes from L's squatting.

DOUBLE (OPTION 2)

L pinches his legs together, locking D's ankle between them. L then penetrates through D's hip while moving both hands to below D's right knee. L used this option because D hopped his left knee under him to prevent the pressure of a dump action.

L will drive both knees in and under

D using the double-knee-drop action as he pulls D's right knee in tight. D will fall to his right side on the mat.

On all of these finishes to a leg attack, penetration is very important. Penetration doesn't just get you to your opponent; it is critical for your option finishes.

FAR LEG TRIP (OPTION 3)

L steps behind D to block D's right leg while still maintaining position on the single leg control. L drives over the posted leg by squatting in and through D. This trips D to the mat for the takedown.

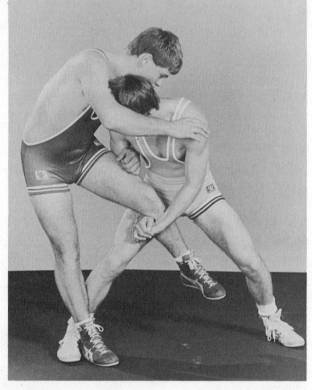

REDUMP (OPTION 4)

L rotates his right shoulder and arm down and through D's hip and thigh. L must pull D's left ankle tightly into his body to maintain control. L's right hip rotates into D as L begins to move his left leg

off and away from D. This redump action goes in the direction opposite that of the dump option. Remember, let your opponent's reaction determine how you move.

If the pressure is good and D was really pulling away, L will end in control of D's leg with D on his hands on the mat. L then maintains control of the ankle and chops D's knee from behind with his right hand. As L drives D's leg to the mat, he will release it and penetrate into D's hips for the takedown.

STEP ACROSS (OPTION 5)

L (fig. 1) penetrates his front leg (left) in and across D. L's right arm tightly controls D's left leg. L's right shoulder drives down and through D's thigh. L's left hand posts D's right leg at or below the knee. L's penetration will then drive D to the mat as his knees are forced together. L keeps pressure into D on the mat by driving into him with the hip be-fore moving up D's hips for control. L should not let his hips fall to the mat or his head drop as he moves for control (fig. 2). The penetration on this move must be across and to the front of D. This option will be set up if D tries to push L's head down or if D just protects and waits.

Figure 1

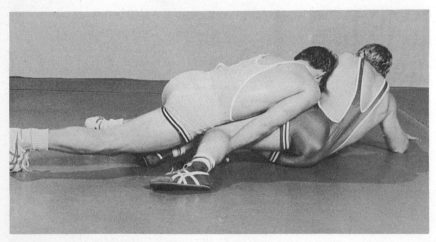

Figure 2

LIFT (OPTION 6)

We can go back to the
Basic Skills chapter for
this position (see page
28, top). You won't be
able to lift if you get out
of position. L finishes the
lift by pulling his arms
across his chest, which
pulls D's knee high and
across L's body. D will
then fall to the mat on
his back and L will as-
sume control.

HIGH HEAD INSIDE SINGLE: LEG TO THE OUTSIDE

The position of control is
the same as with the leg
in the middle. The only
difference is that D
places his lower leg to
the outside of L's right
leg. L continues to pull
D's knee tight to his
stomach. As before, L
must be able to move
about the mat with D's
leg while maintaining his
good stance position.

DUMP (OPTION 1)

L actually lets D's weight settle on his right thigh, as D tries to drive into L. L then moves his right leg back and quickly extends D's lower leg between his, pulling it in and down, as in option one (see page 43, top) from High Head Inside Single: Leg in the Middle.

REDUMP (OPTION 2)

L drives down behind the left knee of D. L also pushes his shoulder forward and into D. The redump here with the leg on the outside is more effective than with the leg in the middle. Look to finish as in option four of the High Head Inside Single: Leg in the Middle section (see page 45).

FAR LEG HOOK (OPTION 3)

L bumps D's knee to his outside and then steps in deep with his right leg. This penetration leg hooks behind D's left leg and drives through for the takedown. This option works if D straightens his controlled leg rather than bending it into L as in previous options.

STEP ACROSS (OPTION 4)

This option is very similar to the step across with the leg in the middle. However, it is easier for L to get deeper penetration across D because D's left knee clears outside L's hip. L still drives his right shoulder down and through D's thigh to finish on the mat.

More experienced wrestlers can elevate the right leg as they step across to block the far knee. Many times D will actually be lifted off the mat in this option. It's good to know it both ways.

LIFT (OPTION 5)

L must let his hands move from control at the knee to high in the crotch. L should not release his grip but should just slide it up the leg. L walks his hip in deep as he straightens up. This lift can finish in the same way as the single lift.

HEAD TIP (OPTION 6)

Many times when the leg is to the outside the attacking wrestler can hip in for a better power position (fig. 1). D has the single here and has brought L's knee high to his chest by hipping into L's leg. The hand lock still stays the same to the inside. If L tries to move in close and pulls his leg to the mat, D can use the head tip option for the takedown (fig. 2). D's right arm releases quickly from L's leg and cuffs L's head, bringing it toward L's knee. D squats and circles backward to D's right, sitting L on his buttocks on the mat.

Figure 1

Figure 2

HIGH HIP OVER (OPTION 7)

L does not pressure into D, but tries to stand his ground. D continues to pull L's right knee high. D rotates his left hip into L, literally pulling L's leg up and over his hip as D circles backward to his left into L. D will finish this option with a knee chop for control (see option four in the preceding takedown on page 45).

HIGH HEAD INSIDE: LEG TO THE FRONT

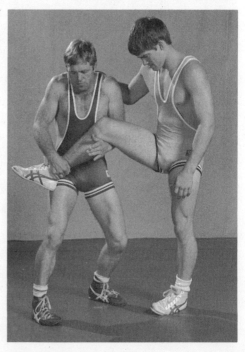

In the photo to the right D has L's leg to the front with the ankle controlled tight to his side with his elbow. The defensive wrestler will not put his leg here. The attacking wrestler must get it to this position.

This next photo shows L moving from a leg in the middle single position by taking D's leg to the front. L's right leg bears the weight as L makes the changeover by dropping his left hand to D's ankle.

DUMP (OPTION 1)

In the photo to the right, D would dump L to his right hip on the mat by squatting and circling backward to D's right. D should apply downward pressure on L's knee as he squats.

FAR THIGH BLOCK (OPTION 2)

As L moves D's leg from the middle of L's legs to the front of L's body, L supports weight on his right thigh and reaches his right arm under D's buttocks, grabs D's right thigh and penetrates through for the takedown.

ELBOW SHOVE FOOTSWEEP (OPTION 3)

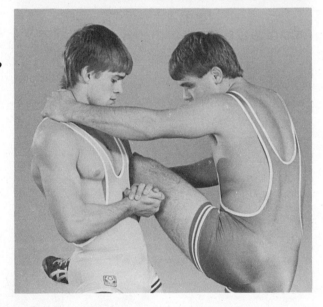

Sometimes the attacking wrestler can move up toward the knee once the leg has been cleared to the front. In the photo above, L has moved to the knee and also moved his hand lock from inside the knee to the same side his body is on. L's right hand drives palm up into his left hand, which holds D's left knee.

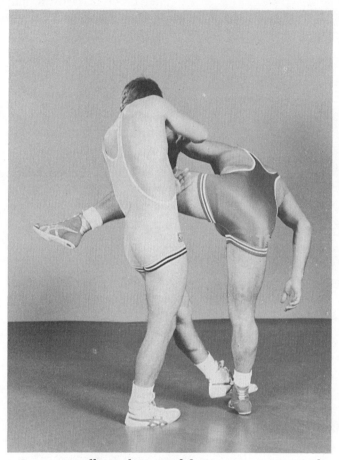

L uses an elbow shove and footsweep option in the photo above to go for the takedown. The footsweep maneuver is used here with L's left leg blocking D's right. L uses his right hand to elbow shove D's left arm in a direction over his posted leg. Again, L may have to finish with a knee chop to gain control. L should be sure to step in deep with his right leg to set up good footsweep position.

It is more effective to learn techniques in a series. The pressure from one option can set up your execution for the next option. But remember: The options work because of the way the defensive wrestler reacts, and his pressure dictates your option.

LOW HEAD INSIDE SINGLE

L has good position on a single leg attack of D on his knees. L pulls

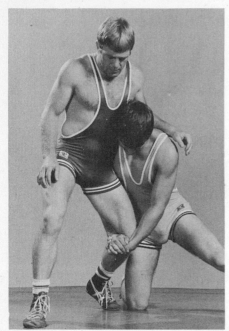

D's knee down toward the mat and into his stomach. L's head is up into D's chest and he has tight control of D's left leg. L's left (inside) hand is still locked under his right to lessen the chance of a counter.

From this position L can drive into D and come to his feet to work all the high single leg options. However, L can work a couple of good options from the low single position as well.

LEG TRAP (OPTION 1)

L keeps as much of an angle on D as he can by moving in a direction into but around behind D's leg to L's right. L always maintains the pressure on D's knee. L shifts his right arm to behind D's far ankle and L drives D forward and across the mat for the takedown.

HEAD UNDER SPLIT (OPTION 2)

D squares up on L and takes away his angle position on the leg. To avoid getting extended under D, L plants his left leg on the mat for a strong post and walks his left knee deep under to drive into D and maintain position (fig. 1). L's right arm still pulls down and in from an outside angle as shown on D's left leg. L can't let his head drop too much. As D continues to drive back in and squares up, L shoots his head between D's legs. While posting on his left hand, he jumps his knees and hips deep under D (fig. 2).

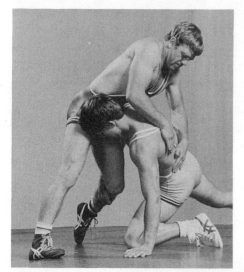

Figure 1

Figure 2

L lifts D up (fig. 3) as his hips continue under and brings his left post hand to drive D's right leg over his head to get the takedown. L's right arm must maintain control and pull down on D's left leg as L elevates the other. L should not fall to his side on this finish, but should pivot on his knees to his right as D rotates off L's shoulders.

Figure 3

HEAD OUT (OPTION 3)

Instead of walking his knee in as in option two immediately above, L rotates his upper body to the side to clear his head from inside of D.

L pulls his right elbow back and high, settling his weight over his own left knee. L then moves his left hand to D's left leg. L will finish the takedown by pulling D's leg and moving around behind him to secure D's right hip or leg.

KNEE PULL (OPTION 4)

L is extended on the mat, but still has pressure down and in on D's knee (fig. 1). As D tries to pull away and extend his own left leg, L drives his head hard into D's stomach and sags and tips toward his right side (fig. 2). L continues to pull down and in on D's knee as he pushes D to his buttocks for control.

Figure 1

Figure 2

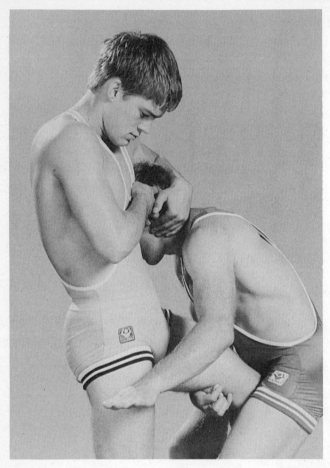

Figure 3

If you're pretty good with all these options on the head inside single both on the feet and on the knees, a smart opponent will move your head from the inside to the outside of his body (fig. 3). As D's head is cleared to the outside of L's body, either D's left hand can come across L's body to a high double position as in the photo, or D can stay on the leg in a head outside single position. A series of options can be worked from both these positions. The defensive wrestler who moves your head will find himself in more trouble if you know these options. Actually, you can move your head inside or outside yourself to make your variety of attack more difficult to defend against. A good wrestler should be able to move quickly from any of the leg attack positions to the others.

HIGH DOUBLE LEG

D must pull L's left leg tight to his hip. D's left arm pulls down and in on L's right hip. D keeps his power position, and as in the single, D must be able to move and adjust without losing his hip power.

DUMP (OPTION 1)

D uses the same backward rotation as in the dump options on the singles. D pulls L's left leg deep between his legs and pressures down harder on L's hip as D squats. D should not go to his knees until L falls to the mat. L sets up this option by driving off his right leg into D.

REDUMP OR FADEOUT (OPTION 2)

L sets up this option by trying to pull his left leg away from D. D follows that by stepping in and arching the hips under at the same time. D should push his head and hips slightly to his left to keep pressure into L. D will pull his left leg out and rotate his hips into L, forcing D to fall forward to the mat.

STEP ACROSS (OPTION 3)

D penetrates across the front of L. As D changes level, his left hand drops to L's right knee to post it. D drives and posts L's right leg as L falls to his right side on the mat with D in control.

LIFT (OPTION 4)

We go back to our skill emphasis for this option. (For photo, see page 27, top, in Basic Skills chapter.) D moves to the side for a more powerful lift with less resistance. D will complete the lift by rotating hard to his left, pulling L down and under him with D's left hand, and penetrating to the mat on his left knee. The rotation should take him through about 180 degrees of motion.

LOW DOUBLE LEG

This is the most commonly used attack in wrestling. L penetrates into D and is on either one or both knees. Many times it is possible to come back up to the feet to the high double, but good options are workable in this low position. L keeps good stance to prevent an easy counter. L pulls down and in on both legs to make D carry L's weight.

STEP ACROSS (OPTION 1)

From this good position, L drives his hips and upper body across in front of D. The head must stay high. L penetrates through on his knee and clamps down hard on D's left knee as L pushes him over that leg.

REDUMP OR FADEOUT (OPTION 2)

L pivots on his right knee and arches his hip in and under D as L rotates to his right. The head is very effective here in bumping D's upper body forward. L pulls D's left leg down to buckle it under as he rotates to finish to his right and rear. L executes this option because D drove down and into him with his hips. The step-across action is to the side. The fadeout is a knee pivot to the side and rear.

LIFT (OPTION 3)

L hips under and loads D on his shoulders. D forced this option by pushing high into L. L will finish by swinging D's knees across to L's left and taking him to the mat.

DUMP (OPTION 4)

L finds himself a little out of position because of D's counter pressure (fig. 1). This, of course, is not desirable, but it will happen. L is

Figure 1

being extended as D drives down and to D's right into L. L rotates his hips to his right and into D, posting D's hip to the mat (fig. 2). L will continue to control D's right leg as L moves more to his right for the takedown.

Figure 2

I have mentioned the importance of changing from one leg attack position to another. Instead of completing this dump option, L could also release D's right leg in the photo on page 65 and move his left arm under D to secure D's left leg in a low single position at the knee. If he gets too extended here, L could go back to the left hand post and knee-walk under as shown earlier in Head Under Split on page 57. He could then work other options there and would have regained a good position. You can see too that if you had a low single with the head inside and your opponent squared his hips, you could also change from the single attack to the double attack. Make these moves flow together.

HIGH HEAD OUTSIDE SINGLE LEG

L controls only one leg and L's head is outside of D. L must keep his pressure in and across D at all times. The head serves as a block and must be kept high. L secures D's leg and buttocks tightly while pulling down and in with his arms. This is the most difficult of the leg attack positions to teach because good stance is absolutely critical to its success.

On all of these leg attack positions, drill over and over again with the attacker first, just trying to keep position while the defensive wrestler tries to force him out of position. If you can't keep good stance, you'll never finish the options against good wrestlers.

LIFT (OPTION 1)

Return to the Basic Skills chapter on page 27, bottom, for this lift. Walk the hips under. L finishes this lift by rotating his hips back to a penetration through D. L pulls D's left leg forward and down as he arches in moving to the penetration.

DUMP (OPTION 2)

L again uses that backward squatting rotation to sit D on his buttocks. This option will be used if D tries to force across L to counter him. L should bring both hands to D's right knee in a quick pulling action to drop D to the mat.

REDUMP OR FADEOUT (OPTION 3)

As D pushes in and tries to pull his controlled leg back, L can hip in and let D's forward pressure take D to the mat. L will pull down on the leg as his hips rotate to his right to provide more pressure.

STEP ACROSS (OPTION 4)

L penetrates back across D while simultaneously moving his right hand to D's left leg to post it. L should try to bring his hand to the front of D's leg, but he may also end up controlling D's calf from the inside if L's right elbow is blocked in by D.

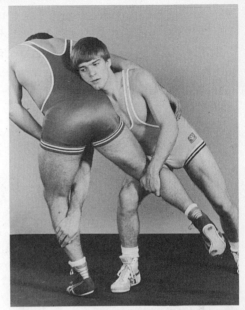

LOW HEAD OUTSIDE SINGLE LEG

There are three distinct positions that can be used when incorporating this low single with the head outside.

In the photo above, D has L's right leg controlled with D's left hand at the knee and D's right hand securing L's buttocks. D pulls in and down to make L carry his weight. Keep the stance!

L isolates hand control onto D's left knee in the second position (fig. 1). This position allows L to pull D's leg more tightly into him.

In the third option L adjusts his control at more of an angle to D and lower on D's leg. L's inside arm controls D's knee while his left arm changes to the ankle. L has shifted his hip more to the left and

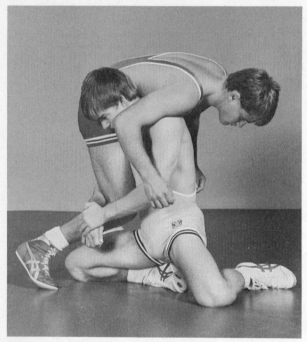

drives his head and shoulders across and into D's right hip. L's driving pressure takes him behind D (fig. 2). D will fall forward and L will pick up the knee and ankle to secure the take-down.

Figure 1

Figure 2

Figure 3

You must practice recovering position. For example, L is in poor position in the photo above (fig. 3) for the head outside single. L must walk his hips in and under D while he pulls down on D's left leg to regain a good position as in figure 1, opposite.

You can practice regaining a power position for all of these leg attack positions.

STEP ACROSS (OPTION 1)

D moves his right knee and hip under L. D's right arm posts L's left leg at the calf and D will drive L to his left hip as he pulls L's legs across his chest to get the takedown.

LIFT (OPTION 2)

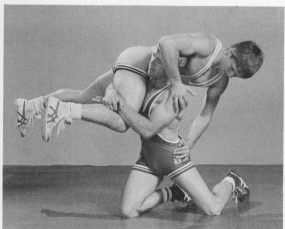

Figure 1

Figure 2

Figure 3

D hipped under and picked L up on his shoulder (fig. 1). This will happen often when L tries to move around to D's right to counter. To finish this lift D moves his right hand across and behind L's left knee and calf (fig. 2). D rotates L's legs parallel to the mat while staying up on his knees. D finishes the takedown by releasing L's right leg and taking that free hand (left) to secure L's lower left leg. D's right hand then becomes free to post across L's body for the takedown (fig. 3). Remember: Keep the head and shoulders high.

DUMP (OPTION 3)

D pulls L's right leg in and under as D sags toward his right hip (fig. 1). D is out of position to a certain extent at the start of this option. L's pressure into D created this recovery option.

Figure 1

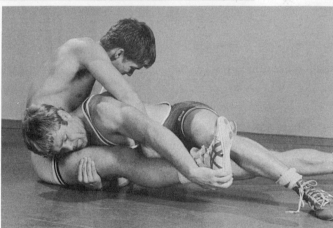

Figure 2

When L falls to his buttocks (fig. 2), D must post L's leg on the mat, keep his head off the mat and drive his hip pressure down and into L. D can keep his left hand at the knee, but moving it to L's heel as shown helps keep L on his buttocks.

D would finish this option by lifting L's right leg high as he shifts his right arm across L's body. D could also walk on his right hip over L's left leg (fig. 3, next page). Note that D settles his weight back across L's leg and does not drive too far forward.

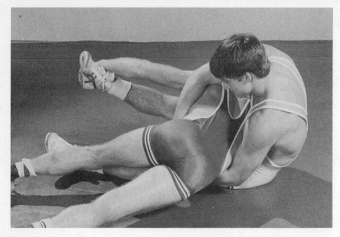

Figure 3

D should not let his hip lie on the mat. His pressure should post L. As D continues to walk his hips and drive around L, he clears his right arm across L's body while his left arm picks up L's left leg as in option two, on page 72, fig. 3.

FIREMAN'S CARRY

Both the arm and the leg of the defending wrestler must be controlled to make this move succeed. L's right arm secures D's leg, while L's left arm pulls down on D's arm. L's hips are in and under D. A good wrestler will realize that many times his shot to this position on another good wrest-

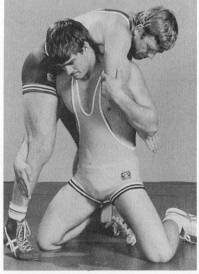

ler will be countered quickly or he must adjust to another leg attack of his own. Either way, L must be able to pivot and change the carry to another attack.

L could easily move from the carry position shown to the right to a head outside single position as in pages 69 and 70. He would simply release D's right arm and square up his own hips and secure D's right leg.

LIFT (OPTION 1)

L's hips move under D as L pulls his left arm down and tips his shoulder on that side down. L elevates his right shoulder, taking D's hips higher than D's head (fig. 1).

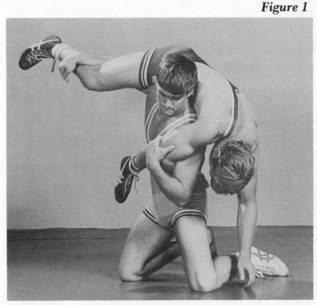

Figure 1

D will drop to his back with L's left shoulder posting D's chest to the mat (fig. 2). L keeps his hips off the mat. L brings his right hand from D's leg to his hip to help L hip heist back to a position facing D.

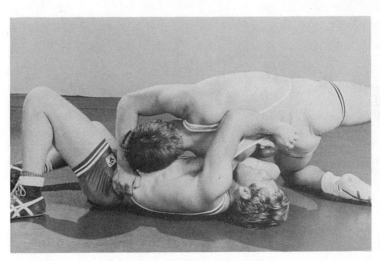

Figure 2

Many times when a wrestler has bad penetration on the fireman's carry, he ends up extended underneath his opponent on his knee. L recovers by using one of two options.

KNEE POST (OPTION 2)

Figure 1

Figure 2

L drives his left knee into D as L pulls down on D's right elbow (fig. 1). Keep that arm controlled. L's right hand blocks across to the outside of D's right knee; D will fall to his back.

Sometimes if D is trying to pull away, L pulls D's shoulder back toward L's knee (fig. 2). This action extends D and L sags to his left hip; D will collapse to his back.

DRAG OUT (OPTION 3)

Figure 1

Figure 2

From the extended-shot position, L swings his hips to the left as his head moves to the right across and under D's chest (fig. 1). L's right arm reaches across to pull D's right elbow while L's left hand first posts on the mat, then reaches over D's back as D is dragged through for the takedown (fig. 2).

HEAD SPIN (OPTION 4)

At times D counters L's carry by clamping tightly on L's head and arm when falling to the mat (fig. 1). L can recover from this stalemate position by maintaining arm and leg control and driving up to a bridge position on his head (fig. 2). By lifting his head and hip heisting, L will gain takedown control.

Figure 1

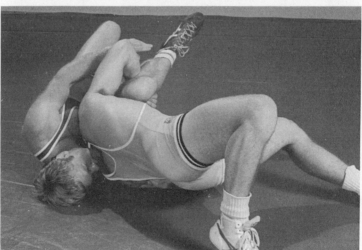

Figure 2

You aim for good hip position on this carry as you would in any takedown attempt. But by quickly using these other options if you get into bad position, you can still get the takedown.

DUCK UNDER

L uses wrist control and squats to move into and under D. L uses knee-over-toe penetration to the outside of D as he ducks his head under the controlled right arm of D. L could also do a duck under by stepping with the other leg. L should not overemphasize raising D's elbow high to the side. Rather he pulls D's arm down and forward and lets D react to set up the duck-under position.

L would use his head to drive behind D's arm and across him to the left. To complete a duck under, L would bring his hips in tight to D and either lift him or move behind him for control. A duck under has many variations, but put simply, it entails squatting under and pivoting around your opponent as you keep pressure into him.

TRIPS AND BLOCKS WITH THE LEGS

At times you must use your legs to assist your upper-body attack. The footsweep and the hip lift emphasize this aspect. Several other techniques are applicable here.

INSIDE TRIP

L sags from an over-under control position on D and moves his left leg inside D's right leg. L bends his knee and rotates his left hip into D so that he can lift his lower leg to block behind D's calf. D is posted over his legs by L's sag and block and will fall to his right hip on the mat. L's head drops down to the outside of D's shoulder as he sags in. In the next photo, L varies this action by dropping his left hand down to D's leg to help block. This inside trip could be done to the other side as well, where L hooks under D's right arm.

OUTSIDE KNEE BLOCK

From the same over-under tie L moves his left leg to the outside and slightly behind D's right leg. L turns his knee into the back of D's leg to post him. L also turns his hip clockwise around D as he sags in behind D, pulling D's upper body over the posted leg. L can use this same action as he locks around D's body.

THROWS

Many throws involve taking your opponent from his feet to his back on the mat. Many wrestlers get hung up in this area of takedowns. Either they feel they don't need them at all, or they force them all the time. Both philosophies are wrong and can create problems for a wrestler.

In reality you will find that variations of the throw attack constitute about 10 percent of the scoring in wrestling. This means you can't force it all the time. It also means if you don't use throws, you miss about 10 percent of the scoring possibilities that better wrestlers use to win.

Five basic skills apply to throws: lifting, the arch and turn, the back step, the hip lift and the footsweep. If you learn these you will be able to take advantage of throw possibilities from any position in wrestling.

These skills give you a reliable sense of where and how to move your hips to attack from any position. You will learn a lot of control tie-up positions in the next chapter. Knowledge and use of these skills will make it possible for you to throw from all of these ties. The combinations of set-ups, ties and throw attacks are limited only by your ability to use the skills and your time and imagination in applying them.

Take a throw because your opponent's pressure provides for it and your skills will guarantee its execution.

Takedowns are essential for effective scoring in all styles of wrestling. If you're going to concentrate on any one area of instruction at the expense of others, make it takedowns. You're much wiser to balance your development, but takedowns can be the key to becoming great.

Chapter 6

SET-UPS and CONTROL TIE-UPS

Every maneuver you make in wrestling has a greater chance of success if your opponent is not really ready for it, or if you are in a position that prevents your opponent's attack until he changes that position. That is what set-ups and control tie-ups, respectively, are all about.

A set-up moves you or your opponent or both into a position that is better for your successful execution of technique. Your set-ups will involve both the upper-body motion and the foot-and-hip motion described earlier. The simplest form of set-up is a head or hand feint in one direction and an attack in another. Fake up and shoot down. Move left and penetrate right, and so forth. Set-ups are as varied as wrestlers in the sport. However, most set-ups involve some type of contact.

A control tie-up is a restraining position that restricts your opponent's attack and facilitates your own attack.

You can set up your opponent with a control tie-up. How he moves to break it or how you move as you control it can also set up your opponent for your attack. Although set-ups can be used from any wrestling position on the feet or on the mat, wrestlers and coaches emphasize these the most in the takedown area.

The more you wrestle and get a sense for the endless variety of wrestling's positions, the more set-ups and control tie-ups you develop. The more set-ups you develop and use, the more successful a wrestler you can become. Remember, mobility is an asset on the wrestling mat. Too many wrestlers slow things down all the time. Keep moving and adjusting from one position to another. Be active.

This won't just happen; you have to work at it. First you must have the stamina to handle the constant repositioning. Second, you must move with a purpose to really make it work effectively for you.

I showed you a variety of takedowns in the last chapter. We need set-ups and control tie-ups, however, to help us to get to those takedown positions.

Set-ups and tie-ups were simplified and put in a unique perspective for me on a trip to the Soviet Union in 1975. I watched a coach in a wrestling club in Tbilisi, Georgia, a southern republic in the USSR, teach young boys about set-ups. Even though I could not speak the language, his actions, repeated over and over again with his young athletes from different contact positions, made his point crystal clear.

Your set-ups and control tie-ups basically move in four directions. They can (1) pull your opponent down; (2) raise your opponent up; (3) take him across your body and away from you; (4) take him across your body and into you. Many times these can work in combinations. Breaking it down this way made it easier for me to picture a desirable action in my own mind. Maybe it can do the same for you.

I'd like to show some common and effective set-ups to start you thinking. I'd also like to emphasize a number of control tie positions that can help make you a better takedown wrestler.

FOREARM BUMP

L uses his right arm to clear D's arm away from his shoulder. This forearm shiver action uses shoulder rotation to bring L's elbow closer to L's side as it bumps D's arm. The bump can be made upward or laterally.

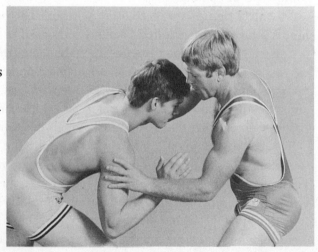

ARM DRAG

Figure 1

Figure 2

L uses his right arm to pull D's arm down and across his body as he penetrates into D with a right leg step (fig. 1). His penetration should cut off D and allow L to gain a leg attack position. The next two photographs show two different ways of initiating this drag set-up. In figure 2, L chops D's hand down at the wrist as he also starts the pull on D's elbow from the inside with his right hand. In figure 3, L circles his left hand to the inside of D's wrist as he bumps it and then circle chops it down to work the same drag position. These hand bumps rotating inside and outside are essential.

Figure 3

HAND CHOP OR SNAP DOWN

D chops L's head down with his right arm high in the neck. The chopping action pulls L down out of position into a position under D. In the next photo, D has extended L with the snap down and D uses his hip to apply more pressure to L's head.

ELBOW SHOVE

L pushes D's right elbow as his right arm controls D's wrist. L forces the arm down into D at the same time he shoves D's elbow across his body. L can then take this set-up into a single-leg attack position.

ELBOW PULL

L punches his right shoulder into D while simultaneously pulling D's elbow tight toward L's chest. D's hand is forced up over L's arm. Note how L's elbow stays low and tight to his side. D does not have any block for a left-side attack by L because of this set-up.

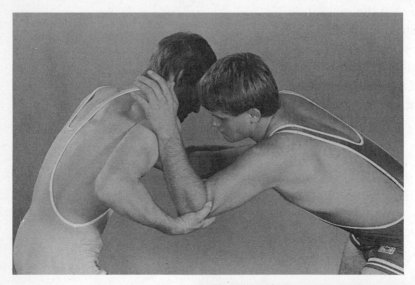

HEAD SHUCK

L rotates his right side into D as he cups his right hand over D's neck. L's left hand reaches for D's elbow with L's thumb hooking to the outside. L then pushes D's head and arm forward and down across his chest as he rotates farther into D. L can move behind D with this set-up action.

These set-ups can be used from an array of contact positions. Remember, you can start these set-up actions and as your opponent reacts to them, you can change to a different set-up and penetrate to a takedown attack position. Combine these with others that you put together from a variety of tie-up situations. Remember that in conjunction with the upper-body adjustments, you must also move your feet and reposition your hips to have effective set-ups, particularly against the better wrestlers.

The set-up actions shown, or variations of them, can be used from a number of different contact or control-tie situations. I believe a good wrestler will use many contact positions. From each of these control ties you must use lots of motion and many set-up variations to give you a versatile and effective attack.

Watch the successful wrestlers and you will also see them go from one control tie-up to another. Many times the change of control tie positions is enough of a set-up itself to effect a takedown.

You must also passively drill these adjustments of position and ties to really get good at them. Train yourself to adjust automatically to varying pressure from your opponent to reflexively use all these set-ups and control tie-ups. Here are some control tie positions for you to look over.

INSIDE OUTSIDE

L and D both have the same arm control position in their tie-up. L's right arm and D's right arm control at the elbow while their left arms control at the bicep. Many times wrestlers start in this position and attempt to work to a tie-up in which both arms are on the inside or both on the outside.

HEAD AND ARM

Again both wrestlers have the same position: Their right arms control each other's head. The elbow should be forced down and in to block the chest and put pressure on the neck. Their left arms control the opponent's elbow. Note that the palm is up and the thumb is to the outside of the elbow.

WRIST AND ELBOW

L controls D's left arm and elbow as in the first two tie-ups. L's left hand controls D's left wrist by grabbing it from the front with L's thumb below D's wrist.

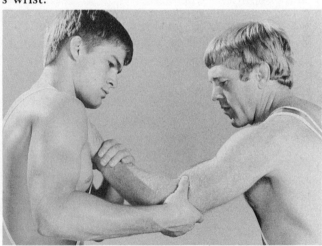

TWO ON ONE ARM

L controls D's right arm with both his arms. L's left arm circles D's arm high toward D's shoulders. L squeezes this arm tightly, locking on the bicep and pulling tightly toward his chest. L keeps his left shoulder higher than D's, pressuring it down and into D. L's right hand squeezes tightly at D's elbow, also pulling down and into his lower chest. L keeps his right elbow tight to his side. Pressure is also applied to D as L sags his left hip down and into D.

Some wrestlers adjust this tie by changing their right arm control from the elbow to the wrist.

In all these ties remember to keep your stance. Don't forget basic skills.

UNDERHOOK

L works for underhook control with his left arm under D's right shoulder (fig. 1). Figure 2 shows an underhook from the back. L controls D's shoulder by keeping his elbow tight, securing his upper arm tightly and pulling in and down at D's shoulder blade. L must keep his shoulder tight and his hip in to keep D away from whizzering (overhooking) his arm and taking away control.

Figure 1

Figure 2

Note: With the underhook control, L must also keep his underhook elbow in close to his side and block off D's free side arm.

FRONT HEADLOCK

D controls L's head with his right arm by squeezing his right arm in and under while controlling L's chin with a slight rotating pressure. D's right shoulder pressures tightly into L's upper shoulder and the back of his neck. D controls L's right arm at the elbow by pulling it forward and into his chest. D can lock his hands in this front head-lock to add additional pressure and control. D does not lose chin control. He locks his right hand palm up and left palm down. L's elbow still is maintained forward. D uses his head for control by keeping it tight into L's arm and shoulder.

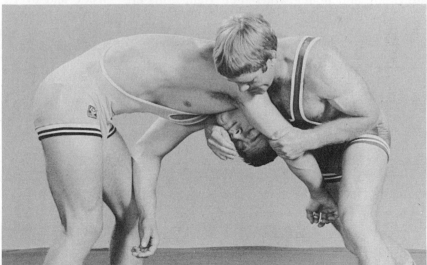

INSIDE TWO ON ONE

L controls D's left arm from the inside. L's left arm circles D's arm high, driving tight into the armpit and securing on the tricep. L's left elbow forces into D's chest for more pressure, and also serves as a block. L's right arm secures behind D's elbow and pulls in tightly. L also squeezes his right elbow tight to block out D's lower right arm. L can alternate between pushing and pulling on this arm to set up his attack. He must control the arm tightly and use his hips for additional pressure.

OVER UNDER

Once again both wrestlers have the same position. Their left arms are inside and under while their right arms are outside and over.

The underhook arm secures on the lower lat muscle and pulls in and down. Do not sink this arm too deep. The elbow of the left arm also forces up into the other wrestler. The right overhook arm pushes down and to the inside on the other wrestler's elbow. Do not lean too hard with chest pressure. Keep good stance at all times. Don't let the head get too high. Keep it down and into the shoulder from the side, not above it.

If you are going to be good with your control tie-ups you have to work on the following. Drilling is essential.

- Move from one control-tie position to another as you make contact with your opponent.

- Move from one control-tie position to another as you move and adjust, or as your opponent moves and adjusts.

- Maintain good position and optimum control while in the tie-up. Some tie-ups give wrestlers identical control. The wrestler assuming the better position and movement will win.

- Set up takedowns from the control-tie positions. You gain no points for getting the tie-up. You must be able to use control-tie positions and tie-ups in combination to gain attack positions that will allow you to score.

A control tie-up does not have to be maintained very long to be effective. All of these tie-up positions can get you into numerous takedown maneuvers shown in the previous chapter. As you get accustomed to a tie-up, you can put together an endless variety of options for attack. You must be able to do two or three from every control-tie position. You can score depending on how your opponent reacts to your motion and pressure as well as your particular control-tie.

As an example, I'll show three options from the underhook, front headlock and over-under tie-ups.

From the underhook:

Figure 1

- L drops to a single leg, because D keeps his left leg in deep driving into L. L's right arm drops from the underhook shoulder control to the leg as he squats (fig. 1).

- L pivots to an inside knee drop, outside step penetration off the underhook (fig. 2). This is set up as D pulls his left leg away to square up with L. L's right arm keeps D's shoulder posted as his head rotates through the leg attack.

Figure 2

- D's weight is posted onto his left leg as L drives into the underhook position. L continues to drive high and across with his shoulder as he steps across D to post the far knee (fig. 3).

Figure 3

From the front headlock:

Figure 1

• As D drives down
into L, pressuring
onto the head, L
posts his legs un-
der to keep from
going to his knees
under D. D drives
over the posted left
leg to secure the
far ankle (fig. 1).

• D pressures L to
his knees and L tries
to pull his back away
to clear his head
out. D releases L's
elbow and headlock with
his left hand and
shucks across L's
head with his
right arm. D
drives his hips
into and to the
right of L (fig. 2).

Figure 2

• L tries to post on his
hands and knees to
maintain position or
to prevent the
first two options.
D maintains control
with the front headlock,
moves his right leg
up and blocks L's
right post arm (fig.
3). D then can pivot
into L's hips for
control.

Figure 3

From the over-under:

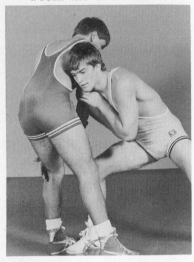

Figure 1

- L drops and penetrates to a leg attack on D (fig. 1). L's right arm posts D's left leg as he drives off the over-under tie-up. L's left hand would drop to D's right leg for a double-leg finish.

- L steps into a footsweep position on D. L pulls down on D's left arm and elevates D's right arm as he posts D over his foot (fig. 2).

Figure 2

- L steps into a body-lock position to his underhook arm side (fig. 3). The hands are locked in this over-under position. L's right leg and hip trap D's left leg.

Figure 3

Variation and effectiveness with these set-ups and control tie-ups is limited only by your imagination and your willingness to work to perfect them. Get into these positions. Use all your skills, and react to your opponent's adjustments.

Chapter 7

COUNTERS to PHENETRATION

A total wrestler is very aggressive in his attack on his feet, but he must also be effective at stopping the attack of his opponent. This ability to counter penetration will require an emphasis of the basic skills. As your opponents use hip power to attack you, you must use your hip power to counteract them.

I have always taught countering penetration after teaching takedown set-ups and tie-ups because I believe it's easier to counter than it is to attack. If a wrestler learns countering first, many times he waits for attack and is not as aggressive a wrestler as he should be.

Get very good at your offense so it's established before you try to defend against all attacks. As you learn to counter it should have a positive effect on your own attack. You learn what works well defensively and this will dictate how you will approach your attack. You know what you have to beat.

I will concentrate, in discussing countering, on the takedown attack to the legs, since this represents more than 90 percent of the attack in wrestling. However, I will first make some comments on countering upper-body attack.

Any time you lean into your opponent and place yourself in a bad stance you can be thrown with some type of upper-body action. Watch the better wrestlers and you'll find they don't get thrown very often. Their stances are good. Their hips represent their center of gravity. They are very good at changing their hip level to thwart the throw attempts. Many times their hip adjustment to counter a throw puts them in a position to execute their own throw. Throws can be used against the good wrestlers, but they must be set up almost perfectly to get a good wrestler out of position.

Learn the lifting, footsweep, hip-lift, arch-and-turn and back-step skills. Many times you will get thrown simply because you don't know how to throw. Many times throws are your best counters to attack.

LEG TAKEDOWN COUNTERS

When another wrestler shoots to a particular leg attack position, you should presume that he is fairly good at that attack. Therefore, one of the most effective counter actions you can make is to change his head position entirely. This will change his leg attack position as well.

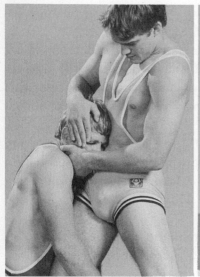 

Figure 1   *Figure 2*

In the above photo (fig. 1) L pushes his hips into D as he covers his hands on D's head to push D's head to the outside of his leg. As he throws D's head to the outside across his leg, L penetrates into D. In the next picture (fig. 2), L continues to push through D after forcing D's head outside. L also blocks D's right arm with his left hand.

The neck is one of the weakest parts of the body, so it makes sense to initiate your counters against the head and neck area. If D were to attack with the head outside, L would move D's head inside with similar action.

Most wrestlers learn to counter leg attacks by throwing their own legs and hips backward away from the attack and dropping the head and shoulders over the attacker. Many times this sprawl action actually gives the attacking wrestler a better opportunity to finish because the hip power of the counter wrestler is diminished. In all of these counter actions, it is imperative that your hips drive down and in to the attacker. At the same time, your head and shoulders must remain high. Your legs can pull away, but not your hips. Arch your back as you drive your hips to counter.

The most effective way to stop your opponent's penetration is to create your own penetration. You can only do this with hip power. As you wrestle and keep good position, you will find you have some good blocks to your opponent's penetration as he begins to attack.

Figure 1

In the photo above (fig. 1), L posts his head in D's chest to create a temporary block of any leg attack. Don't compromise your stance by bending too far to use his head block. But good wrestlers are very effective with it.

In the next photo (fig. 2), D attempts a shot, but L changes level and posts with his hands to prevent D's penetration. L's hips drop as he drives to stop D.

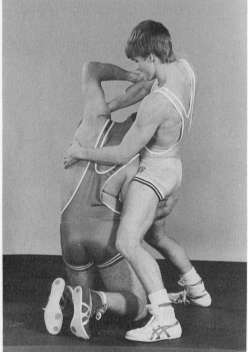

Your opponent will set you up and penetrate into you no matter how good a wrestler you become. If he gets in deep, your hips can still stop the action. In the photo to the left (fig. 3), D has taken a good fireman's carry shot into L. The fireman's carry attempts to control the upper and lower body simultaneously. Your counter action must be dependable to beat it.

The counter action we will demonstrate for leg attacks in this chapter centers on the action demonstrated here to beat the fireman's carry attack.

L drives his hips down and into D, changing the angle of his counter by rotating the hips to the side and arching his back as he lifts his head and shoulders high to help clear the arm. L extends his arm and pulls from his shoulder to clear it.

This counter action incorporates a lot of reaction into one counter. I've found it's a good one to drill right away since it gives the wrestlers a real sense of what they have to do to be effective with countering. You can't sprawl away and lose your hip power. You must drive your hips in and down to crush the attacker. You've got to use those skills we discussed earlier.

The leg attack is quite varied. You need to be able to adjust and counter all possible variations. Let's show some options for counters from a number of leg attacks.

ELBOW LIFT

As D penetrates into the double-leg position, L blocks out his left arm at the elbow. L's hips drive down and in. L's left arm squeezes D's head and upper arm. By rotating his hips into D and lifting and driving on D's elbow, L can drive D to his right hip for control.

HIP WALK-OVER

Figure 1

This can work on both a low double leg and a low head outside single leg. As L penetrates (fig. 1), D puts his right hand on L's head and drives it into the mat. D's hips drive down and into L. D's left hand pushes across L's lower rib cage and helps drive L to his left shoulder (fig. 2). As L drops, D posts his right hand to keep from falling on his own hip. D's legs and hips drive into L. (Note: Don't pull the legs or hips back or you will fall to your hip and get taken down.) D finishes the counter by walking his hips all the way around L for control. D's hip weight stays on L throughout this entire counter.

Figure 2

CROSSFACE

L demonstrates an effective crossface counter maneuver on D (fig. 1). D's head is
rotated and lifted by L. Most wrestlers try
to drive the head to the side, which is not as
effective. Lift the head, since the neck is
not as strong in that direction as it is pushing across into you.

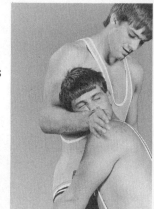

Figure 1

Figure 2   *Figure 3*

In the photo above (fig. 2), D applies a crossface to counter L's
low head outside single-leg attack. Note how the hips drive into L
low as D's arm lifts L's head. The next photo (fig. 3) shows D finish-
ing the counter with a hip-sag headlock after crossfacing the head.
D continues to lift the head all the way across his body as D rotates
his hips for the throw.

HIP CUTOFF

As L penetrates into D, D pushes down on L's head (fig. 1). At the same time, D rotates and drives ninety degrees with his hip into L to cut off L's penetration. D changes his angle and his altitude at the same time.

Figure 1

In the next photo (fig. 2), L uses the hip cutoff and takes a crossface position on D's head instead of pushing it to the mat. L secures D's far arm (left) and from this position would drive D to his left hip and shoulder on the mat.

Figure 2

HIP OVER

Instead of driving to L's right across the attacking wrestler as has happened in all the previous counters, L uses a hip over to pull D to his opposite hip. L's right hand controls D's shoulder while his left hand controls D's upper right arm. L uses a hip sag to put additional pressure on D to drop him to his back on the mat. L posts his right arm to the mat to allow D to fall underneath him. This also keeps L from dropping to his hips and shoulder.

HIGH CHEST LOCK

Figure 1

As D penetrates, L squares up with D, locking his hands high in D's chest, posting D's head under L's lower chest (fig. 1). L squeezes his elbows together, extending D's arms forward. As L drives his hips down, D will put his hands on the mat to keep from falling to his head on the mat. When this happens, L moves his left leg up and around D as a block. L still maintains control of D's arms (fig. 2). L continues to drive into D as he moves behind him for control. L's left hand will move to D's left hip and his right hand will secure D's head as L moves behind D.

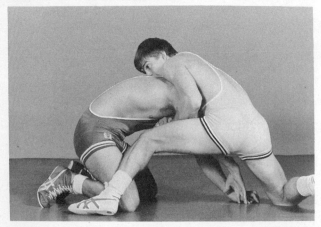

Figure 2

SHORT DRAG

Figure 1

L attacks with a single leg on D. D first pushes L's head down and drives his hips into L's right shoulder. D's left hand and elbow control across on L's left hip. D then works his right hand between L's body and head to secure L's upper right arm (fig. 1). D continues to drive down and into L with his hips. As he drags the arm forward he moves around behind L (fig. 2). Note that D does not cross his legs over to walk behind L. D's hips must stay as square to L as possible and drive into L to post his weight on his hands.

If L is very persistent and strong, and it is difficult for D to get his

Figure 2

hand inside L's head, D shifts his hips and hand position and moves for control by driving to the opposite side of L (fig. 3). D's right hand moves off L's head and to L's right hip. D's left hand moves from L's hip to his right elbow as D changes hip pressure into L. D's right hip rotates into L as he moves to his left around L. This hip pressure posts L to his right shoulder as D drives around L (fig. 4).

Figure 3

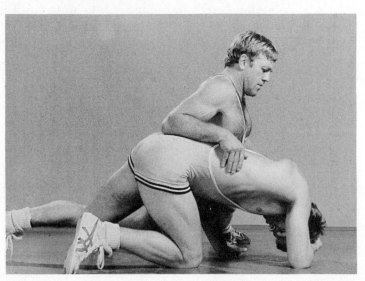

Figure 4

KNEE ROTATE AND SIT

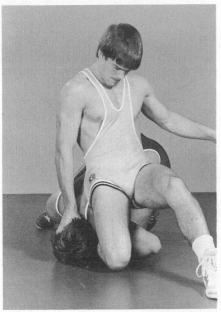

If D takes a low single-leg attempt, many times it is safer for L to post D's head to the mat and sit on his shoulder (fig. 1). L should not let his right knee make prolonged contact with the mat or he loses his pressure into D. L drives back off his left leg, pushing low into D.

Figure 1

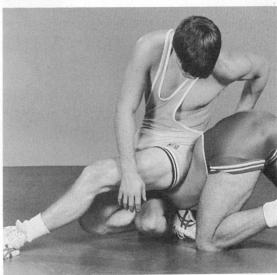

Figure 2

In the photo above (fig. 2), L begins to rotate back toward D's hips. Note that L's right instep is facing the same direction he is turning. L's left hand grabs D's right hip as L pivots. L's weight drives into D's shoulder and back as he spins.

L can come around to secure D's ankle as his own right leg rotates clear from D's control (fig. 3). L must keep his weight settled on D for this finish.

Figure 3

LIMP LEG

By pushing down on D's head, L can many times take D to the mat to finish options already described. However, wrestlers must learn other options for the high leg attack.

The limp leg is a great counter action for the high leg attack. L starts the limp leg action by getting his knee higher than his own hip. He forces into D to loosen the leg so he can rotate the knee down and the heel up. L then pulls the leg down and forward from the hip to clear the leg from control. Remember, keep the pressure on the head.

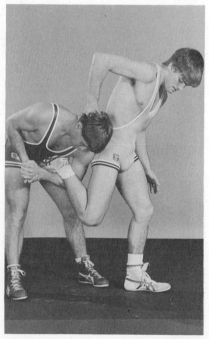

HEAD AND ELBOW POST

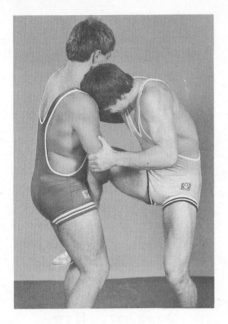

L counters a high single by driving his head high into D's head and chest at the same time he drives his controlled leg hard toward the floor. He then pulls in and down on D's elbows. The pressure generally clears the leg.

HEAD POST AND ELBOW PULL

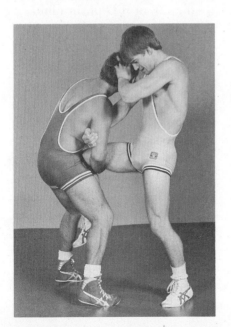

Again L has the high single, grabbing D's right arm high with his own right arm. L's left arm forces D's head to the outside. L then drives his body down and into D as he drags the arm and shoulder across his chest. L's left arm will drop to D's body to help drive D to L's right.

RECOVERY ON THE MAT: HAND POST

Figure 1

Figure 2

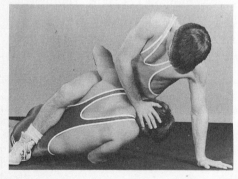

Figure 3

I show this counter action because wrestlers often relax or assume improper hip position when they feel they have scored. You can take advantage of this laxity to counter. In the photo to the left (fig. 1), D has almost completed a double-leg takedown, but his hips are not pressuring down and in, and his head and shoulders are low. L posts up off his left hand, driving his hips back into D. L's right hand posts on D's head to keep it out of position.

Depending on D's reaction, L can rotate his hips and clear from D's control (fig. 2), or if D pushes into him, L can move his right leg high into D and turn him right to his back (fig. 3).

Wrestlers should learn to post their hands and elevate their hips (remember the basic skills?) from any leg attack position in which they might get driven to the hips.

Countering penetration effectively can make you a great wrestler. Work on moving your opponent's head first to change his position every time your opponent attacks. Then the counter actions in combination can make you very difficult to take down.

Chapter 8

ESCAPES and
REVERSALS

Wrestling rules provide for action in the referee's position on the mat. One wrestler starts on his hands and knees in the down referee's position. The other wrestler in the up referee's position begins with control of the down wrestler with one hand on his opponent's elbow and the other hand around his waist. A good wrestler in the top position can make it almost impossible for you to get away or reverse position. You need to give yourself as much advantage as you can to make scoring from this position feasible. If you can't make things happen from the down referee's position, you can really limit your overall success.

The biggest mistake most wrestlers make here is in letting the top man initiate the action and then trying to counter him. This can be and often is disastrous. You'll improve your success ratio from the bottom if you move first, move hard and keep moving.

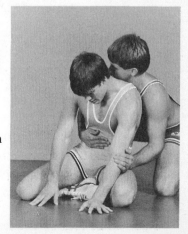

As in every other wrestling technique, position is everything. Your stance and hip power are vital. It is imperative that you move to a hip power position and quickly execute an option right on the whistle.

In the photo to the right, L, in the down referee's position, pushes back into D to a good power position, settling over his left hip and leg. Do not settle the hip or buttocks on the mat. L keeps his head up, his elbows in and his hips underneath him. Getting extended forward with too much weight on your hands is as bad here as in your takedown attack.

When you move into this position off the whistle, keep pushing backward and low into your opponent. As the top man pressures back into you, move your knees and shift your hips to keep good position.

This knee movement for hip adjustment is what I call skating. It's all an effort to maintain a position of power. From this position you can move to an escape or reversal as you react to your opponent's pressure from behind. You can prevent a wide variety of rides from this good base.

THE STAND-UP

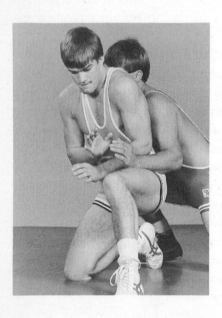 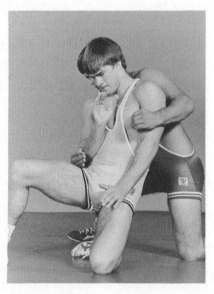

The most widely used technique from the down position is the stand-up. It should be one of your best moves. You'll find as you drive and settle over your hip using the skating technique that you will take the weight off the other leg. Any time this happens you can move that leg up to begin your stand-up. The above pictures show L doing an inside and outside leg stand-up, respectively, with D riding to the left.

The key in the stand-up is to push back and drive into the top man. Don't step forward and away. Push back and keep that stance. Adjust and rotate the hips to keep balance. Note how in both positions L keeps his elbows in tight to maintain hand control. If D can lock his hands as L comes up, the stand-up won't work very often.

As L pushes up on one leg, driving his head and shoulder into D, he can clear his other leg out to come to his feet. In this position L must still keep his elbow in and settle his hips down and back into D. Don't walk forward. Push back. With proper pressure, L looks as if he is sitting in an invisible chair.

If D tries to pull L to his back, L should be prepared to do a hip-heist maneuver to recover (see page 37–38 of the Basic Skills chapter). When doing the hip heist, L can post to his elbow or at times can twist through quickly and post immediately to his hands and knees for the escape.

If D comes up to his feet with L, L continues to push back into D. L can pop his hips forward and cut his arm through D's tight waist arm. L moves his right leg back behind his left as he pivots to face D. This should be done quickly and explosively. A good wrestler can take advantage of this pivot position by driving right back into penetration attack under D.

Let's take a look at some adjustments that can be made if you come to your feet without good hand-control position.

L has let D's left arm get underneath his left elbow (fig. 1). L's right elbow is in tight and L uses that hand coming from close to his chest to block above D's left hand. As he pushes D's hand down and out, he brings his left elbow back tight inside to regain good hand-control position (fig. 2).

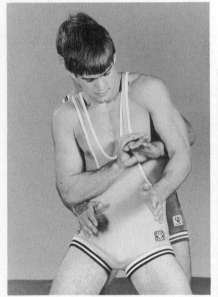

Figure 1

Figure 2

D has gotten inside L's left elbow and locks his left hand high under L's left shoulder (fig. 3). L keeps his right forearm and elbow as tight as possible and covers his chest with that hand. L reaches up with his left hand to grab D's hand. L can use his right hand coming tight across his chest to assist in pulling D's hand down and extending it, and post it to his left hip (fig. 4). From here L can pivot and cut out for the escape.

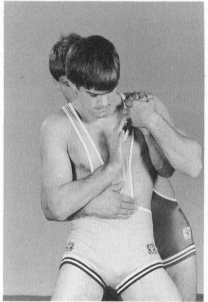

Figure 3

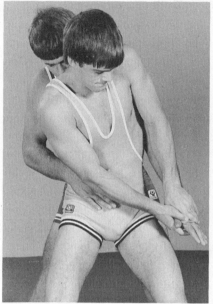

Figure 4

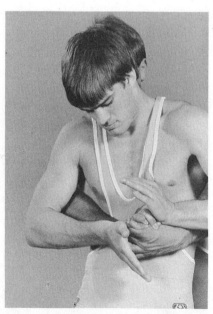

Figure 5

D has locked his hands around L (fig. 5). L can use the heels of his hands to push in opposite directions across D's finger grip to break the hand lock. L should drive down and out with his hands as he keeps good hip and back pressure.

D has both hands inside and has secured two-on-one wrist control (fig. 6 next page). L pries his right arm inside to clear D's right hand off his wrist. When it clears, L uses his left hand to block it out. L then brings his right elbow back in tight to his side to clear D's entire right arm, as on p. 118.

L then posts his right hand across on D's left hand. L straightens his left arm and could clear D's left hand as he did previously above. You don't have to grab a hand to have control. Just keep your elbow tight.

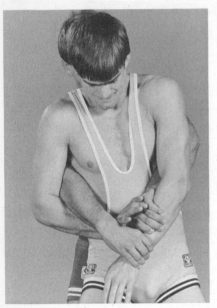

When you get the stand-up position, apply these three rules and you'll be more successful with it: (1) don't bend over; (2) don't walk forward; (3) don't clear your elbows from your side until you pivot.

When you push back to good position, you may find some other escapes and reversals set up as the top man tries to beat your stand-up.

Figure 6

NEAR ARM ROLL

L grabs D's right waist arm with his right hand. He can control the wrist or control the hand. L pushes back to his right elbow, driving into D with his back. L helps push D with his left elbow forcing into D's left shoulder.

As D falls to his side, L grabs D's right leg and secures both his hands on D's right wrist, gaining the reversal and probably some back points. L rotates his hips square to the mat but does not let his hips rest on the mat.

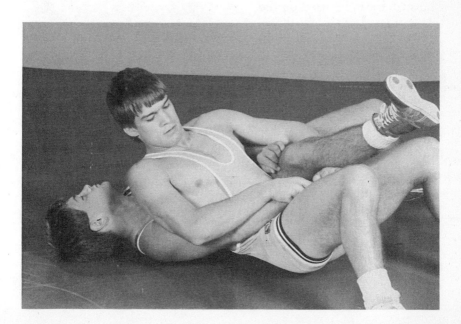

CROSS ARM ROLL

As L pushes back, D's pressure is more across L's body so L must keep his right arm posted for support. L grabs D's right tight waist arm with his left hand. L again drives backward until D collapses to his side where L can change to the same finish as in the near arm roll. Don't fall forward on this roll. Drive back and to the side. Both

the near and cross arm rolls can be used from the feet as well. These are also good options to use when you are countered back to the mat after standing up.

SWITCH

The switch can be used on the mat and on the feet just like the roll. Here L starts the switch action on D while on his feet. As L drives back into D, L rotates and sags to his right. L's right arm posts over D's right elbow and L's hand grabs inside D's right knee and thigh. L will continue to pivot his right knee into D as he pulls D's thigh and drives his right shoulder down and across. This action will bring him behind D for the reversal. Keep your weight down and into your opponent.

LEG LIFT-OVER

L grabs D's left leg at the ankle and lifts it back over his hips. This was set up because D drove his left knee onto L's left thigh as he worked to control L. L would finish by continuing to lift D's leg, posting more weight on his right arm and elevating his own hips to complete the leg lift. L should turn to his right, facing into D, who would fall off L to the rear. Don't spin toward the leg you are lifting, turn away to face him.

WHIZZER

L overhooks D's left arm with his right arm. L sags his hip down and into D as he angles forward. L's right arm also pulls tightly into his side to keep D's arm secure. L pushes off his left arm to add

Figure 1

Figure 2

pressure into D. Sometimes L can lock his whizzer arm onto his own thigh for good pressure.

L's whizzer pressure can drive D onto his side (fig. 1). From here L can circle up to D's head for a reversal and apply a pinning combination (fig. 2). When you put in a whizzer, keep your arm tight and force down more into your opponent than you pull forward. A whizzer can also be used effectively on the feet to counter attacks. If you don't emphasize this type of pressure, you can lose the whizzer to a wrestler who knows a good limp-arm technique.

L begins a limp-arm action on D. L rotates his own palm to position it for the limp-arm action (fig. 3). To free his arm, L pulls forward, letting his arm drop down and across D's side as he drops his hip into D (fig. 4). To limp-arm effectively, L pulls from the shoulder and lets his arm swing through. As his arm clears, L will pull back and raise his right arm over D to gain the reversal control.

Figure 3

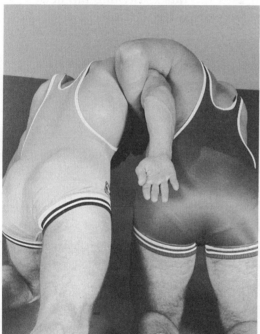

Figure 4

This limp-arm technique can be used any time you want to free your arm from control from one of a host of positions. Shift or swing the arm from the shoulder to clear it. Move your hips into your opponent.

ELBOW POST

I want to re-emphasize the hip-heist action that can be used so often to score.

D tries to break L down to his side. Instead of falling to his hip and shoulder, L posts his left elbow forward and drops his hips back into D (fig. 1). L keeps his right hand tight to his side. He elevates his hips to begin the hip-heist action. L's right arm scrapes D's right arm off his waist (fig. 2). L then uses the quick, twisting hip-heist action to rotate away from D for the escape (fig. 3)

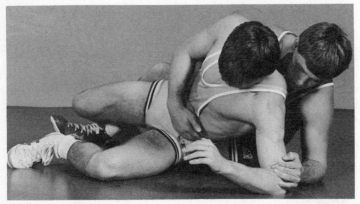

Figure 1

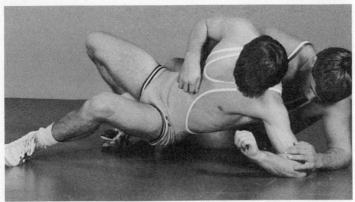

Figure 2

The stand-up will be your bread-and-butter escape and reversal move. But the other options shown can also put points on the scoreboard for you as you find the opportunity to use them.

Figure 3

Figure 4

Keeping a good base position if you're on the bottom is the key to your success. If you get broken down to your stomach, push back over a knee and get good position quickly. In the above picture, L drives his weight over his right knee to recover his base. When pushing up, L will need to keep his elbows in tight to block off D's attacks. As quickly as possible both of L's knees must be recovered underneath his hips or he will be broken down again.

Wrestlers who are good on top will put in leg rides. We will cover these in the next chapter. Legs are hard to put in if you are in a good bottom stance.

If D starts to put a leg in, L can drop his hip on that side, extending his own leg, and post his weight on D's leg. L must push backward as he extends his left leg. He will clear his knee back inside off D's leg and again recover a solid, sound base.

On occasion, wrestlers will get pulled back into what is called a crab position in the lap of the offensive wrestler. L reacts to this position by posting on his hands and elevating his hips. L should not drive his back and head into D's chest. This will get him turned on his back. L steps on D's right leg, posting it, and walks and settles his hips out over D's legs. L will end up perpendicular to D in control as in the photograph on page 121, bottom. L's hips stay off the mat. If you can't make this hip action work for you, turn back to your base on your hands and knees and start fresh. You've got to be able to score quickly from the bottom. Learn these fundamental maneuvers and positions so your down wrestling can enhance your chance for success.

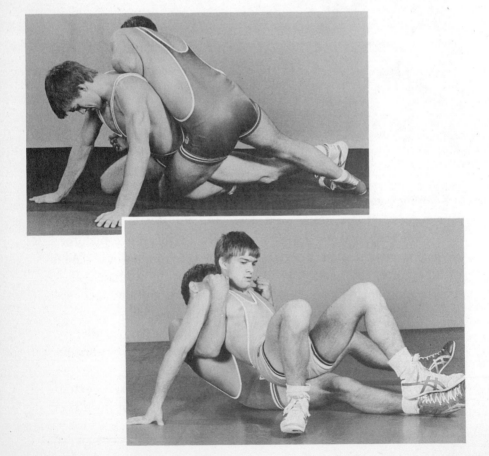

Chapter 9

RIDES and BREAKDOWNS

Once you have taken your opponent down, you want to maintain that control and ultimately work to turn him to his back. Make the other wrestler work hard to escape and keep position that will prevent giving anyone a reversal. As you maintain control you can wear your opponent down.

You can take two or three control positions and make them work on everyone you wrestle. You don't need as varied an attack here as in the takedown area. Rides and breakdowns should be used for aggressive action. You want to control so you can turn your opponent to his back. Don't use these maneuvers to prevent scoring and stall. A good ride should take you to pinning situations.

When you start on top in the referee's position, learn to clamp your legs tightly to bind your opponent. In the photo above, L squeezes his knees together, catching D's ankles and posting him.

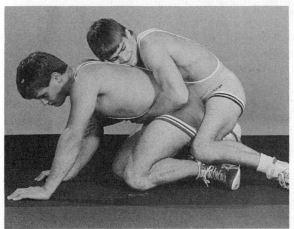

The positions in this chapter can be very effective for you in controlling your opponent. The pinning situations that can develop from these rides and breakdowns will be covered in the next chapter.

SPIRAL

The spiral ride is currently the most effective control and breakdown position in high school and college wrestling. L drives his left hip forward and sags it to the side of D. L's left arm drives under and across D's chest as L's forearm pressures forward through D's left arm. L's left hand is across D's chest, or he can hook it on D's right trapezius. L runs his hips forward and into D, driving through D's shoulder. L's right arm pulls down and in, wrapping in on D's right thigh.

A variation of this spiral that is also very effective is the spiral half on next page. L reaches his left arm under D's left arm and over his neck. To get this position L may drive his head into D's head to push it down. The hip position and rotation is very similar to the regular spiral although L pulls down more on the half nelson with his left arm. L gets the best pressure on these spiral options if he stays pretty much hip-to-hip with D and drives down with the inside right hip. If D drops his right shoulder, the half nelson can turn him

to his back. L helps to break D down by driving his right knee into D's left thigh. This prevents D from being able to recover his hips under him as L spirals.

TIGHT WAIST

Figure 1

Figure 2

L chops down on D's left arm and squeezes tight around D's waist with his right arm (fig. 1). L tries to pull D's hips and elbow together. L also uses his left knee to block D's left knee so he can pull him over the post to break him down (fig. 2). Many times this takes D right to his back or he fights to his stomach to avoid the turn.

FAR ARM TRAP

L clamps D's left elbow as in the tight waist. As L blocks the elbow into D he secures it at the waist across D's body with his right arm (fig. 1). L then drives forward into D and shifts his hips to the opposite side of D, keeping the arm trapped (fig. 2).

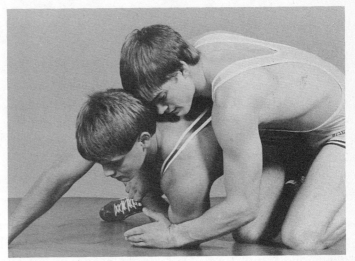

Figure 1

Figure 2

TURKEY BAR OR ONE-ON-ONE

Figure 1

L can take this ride off either the spiral or the tight waist start. L's left hand secures D's left wrist (fig. 1). L drives his left shoulder down and forward into D. L's right hand controls D's right hip to break him to the mat. L drives D's chest to the mat as he moves perpendicular to D (fig. 2).

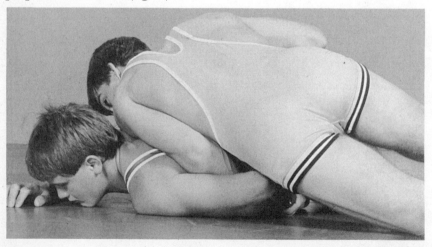

Figure 2

ANKLE RIDE

L shifts his hips over to the same side of his tight waist arm. He picks up D's left ankle and drives at an angle toward and across D. This pressure will break D down to his left hip. As L drives he can drop his right arm across to D's left thigh or knee. L can also work a similar control breakdown by securing and lifting D's right ankle as well. It is stalling to stay on the ankle too long.

LEG SCOOP

L started his control to the right of D. L scoops and hooks D's right ankle with his left leg. L drops his left arm to D's right leg from behind. He also pulls D's head into him and down with chin control. The head control with L's right arm is very important. L will drive D to his left hip for

the breakdown as he picks up D's right leg. Often this will lead to a cradle pinning combination.

LEG RIDES

Your legs are stronger than your arms so it makes sense to use them to help you control your opponent's hips. The rides shown here should flow together. Use one to get into another. Whenever possible, move your legs in for greater pressure to break your opponent down or hold him down.

Use the following three leg control positions:

LEG FIGURE-FOUR

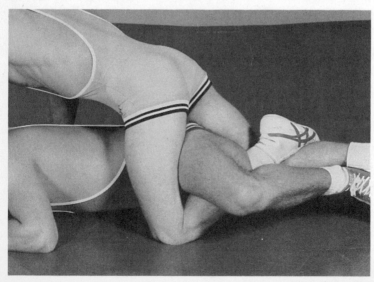

Figure 1

The toe of one leg hooks behind the knee of the other. Get up high on your opponent's thigh. L shows the leg figure-four on D two ways. The outside leg figure-fours the inside leg (fig. 1) and the inside leg figure-fours the outside leg (fig. 2).

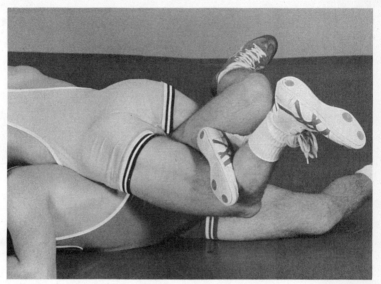

Figure 2

LEG HOOK

The leg blocks or hooks under the opponent's thigh.

LEG LACE

The hook leg laces and posts behind the far knee for greater leverage.

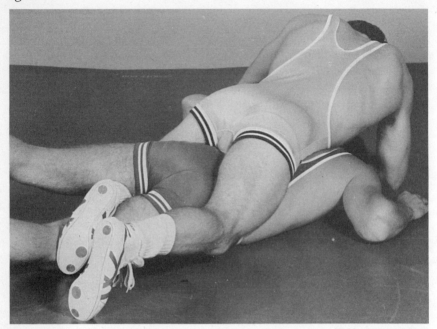

Again, I want to emphasize percentage techniques. You want your leg rides to work on good wrestlers. You can't work legs on good people while lying on your side. Stay above them. Keep your head and shoulders high, arch your hips in and lift with your legs. Your opponent's head should be under your lower chest. Stay high on him for greatest leverage. Whenever you apply the legs, squeeze your knees together. This binding pressure makes leg control effective on the figure-four. You squeeze your opponent's leg on the figure-four, but on the leg hook and the leg lace, you squeeze your opponent's hips together.

Since the bottom man will usually work to get to his feet, we should presume that no matter how good you are with rides and breakdowns, opponents will get to their feet on you. You need to know how to break them back down to the mat.

There are three very effective ways to regain control of a wrestler who has regained his feet and break him back down to the mat:

• Change to a double-leg position and take him back down. In the photo to the right (fig. 1), D has stood up on L. L shifts his head behind D as he rotates his hips toward the side of D. L then drops his level, and moves his hands to D's knees. L penetrates back through D.

Figure 1

Figure 2

• Change to a single-leg position and take him back down. In this photo (fig. 2), L completes this breakdown by shifting his hands and hips to a single-leg attack and penetrates into a good position to work a single-leg option back to the mat.

• Lift the man and footsweep him back to the mat. In this photo (fig. 3), L has locked his hands around D. L applies his footsweep skill after lifting D. L's left knee clears D's body to the side. As D falls, L drops to his knees and pulls D's hips in and under him for control.

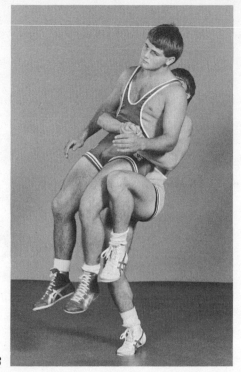

Figure 3

At times in wrestling, if you are good with takedowns, it is certainly to your advantage to release your opponent to go for another takedown. But every wrestler should be able to control his opponent when he has to. Whether you emphasize the takedown or the control is a personal preference. Your relative effectiveness in all areas of wrestling is to a great degree dependent on the learning time you put into a particular area.

My personal approach emphasizes the takedown, to facilitate a changeover to international wrestling rules, which do not provide for long control periods. I also think wrestlers can get much better overall by working takedowns than they can by riding.

As a wrestler or coach you need to make your own decision. Whatever you do, be aggressive at it. Change off frequently and look for the turns to the back. Don't be called for stalling because you're just riding. Don't be lazy. Establish good ride and breakdown habits from the start. *Move* and *adjust!*

Chapter 10

PINNING COMBINATIONS

Pinning, holding both shoulders of your opponent on the mat, is the ultimate in wrestling and it's the most exciting thing to watch. You need to familiarize yourself with a number of potential pinning combinations that will give you the opportunity to get the fall or score back points.

Good wrestlers often take their opponents to their backs right from their takedown or counterattack. The throws, which include upper-body maneuvers and leg-trip attacks, almost always mean taking the other wrestler from his feet to his back. If you drill and wrestle with the fall potential in mind, you will try to turn every scoring situation into an effort to put your opponent on his back.

Let's take a look at the holds you can apply to put or keep your opponents on their backs.

Many of these holds can be applied off the takedown, while others require a concerted effort after you have established control and break your opponent down. Whenever they can be used, they are good to have in your arsenal of pinning attacks.

The best way to turn and hold your opponent's shoulders toward the mat is, again, to use the power in your hips. Don't apply pressure with just your arms and shoulders. Let your hip weight work for you. If you take away your opponent's skill positions and you apply your own, your pinning ability will also improve.

Some good pin holds to use are listed here:

HALF NELSON

L drives his left arm under D's left arm and pressures forward and across the elbow. L's left hand cups D's neck high (fig. 1). L's hand serves as the fulcrum for the lever action. L's body moves perpendicular to D and his head and shoulders stay high. L should not drop his head to the mat. Arch the hips in. L can drive his arm deeper around D's neck as he works for the fall. L can use a bicep hook or elbow lift to assist in getting the half-nelson position (fig. 2). L secures his hand and wrist around D's elbow and levers it up and forward. As D turns to his side, L can drop his hand in to secure the half-nelson position. L's legs should move forward and in toward the head as he arches and drives to turn D.

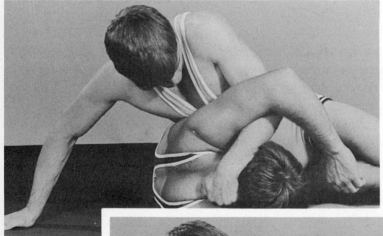

Figure 1

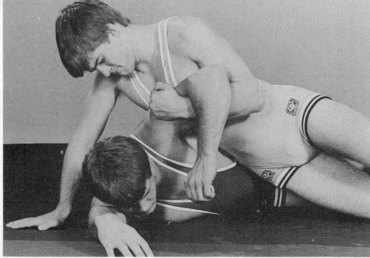

Figure 2

ARM BAR

D's right arm overhooks L's right arm above the elbow and circles D's bicep. D's hand reaches in to clamp on L's right lat muscle or scapula. D must squeeze L's upper arm as he walks his hips perpendicular to L in a direction to post L's left shoulder on the mat. D helps drive and post L by driving down on L's neck with his left forearm. D must keep L's elbow in his right armpit.

In the photo above, D drives L to his back by walking his hips forward and into L. Notice that L's elbow is still secured in D's armpit. D settles his right elbow down alongside L's head. Staying directly above L, D can put additional pin pressure on L by driving L's left elbow forward by scooping it with his right knee and thigh and running it forward. Some wrestlers bar the near arm and half nelson the far arm to force a turn to either side.

LOCKED HALF NELSON

L could come into this position by walking an arm bar all the way over the head. L keeps the bar arm controlled and drives his hips down and in alongside D's head. L uses his right arm to secure a half-nelson position on D's neck (fig. 1). The photo below (fig. 2) shows another view of the locked half nelson. L locks his hands under D's neck toward the arm-bar side. L will use a finger grip lock here with the half-nelson hand turning palm down and the arm-bar hand facing palm up. L squeezes his elbow together, pinching D's head and arm. L's chin should be along D's upper side. Keep the hips low and arched in.

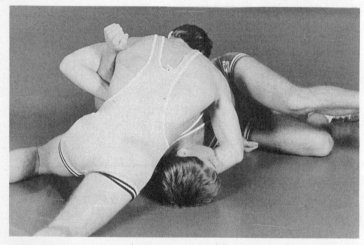

Figure 1

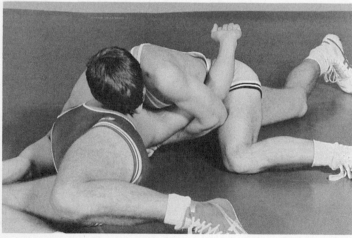

Figure 2

REVERSE HALF NELSON

Instead of reaching his arm under L's arm and going over the head as in the half nelson, D comes over the arm and goes under the head for the reverse half. D's hips move out perpendicular and again crowd D's shoulder and elbow as he arches the hip in and bends the leg forward. D could lift L's elbow with his right arm and lock his hands, bringing L's left elbow and head together.

HEAD LOCK

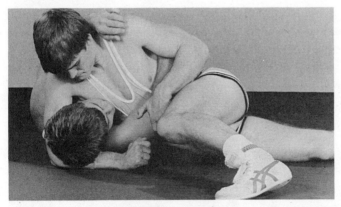

L controls D's head with his right arm and D's left arm with L's left arm. L's left arm lifts D's arm at the elbow. For optimum hip pressure, L should keep his hip square to the mat and drive his left knee in and under his own left arm. He should keep his head and shoulders high. L works to squeeze D's head and arm together as he hips in.

OVER-UNDER PANCAKE

L has an overhook on D's right arm and an underhook on D's left arm and lat muscle. L stays centered over D's chest and moves perpendicular to D, moving his left leg forward and into D to help elevate D's right arm forward. L can lift D's left arm to clear D's elbow from his side.

FACELIFT

L could sink in a deep half nelson here but takes the facelift instead. L's left arm cradles D's head. D's chin is tight in L's inside elbow while L's arm makes contact all along the side of D's face. With L's hand clamping on top of D's head, L lifts D's head toward D's right shoulder. L's right arm is under D's left arm. L should bind D's head and left arm together as he hips into D's chest.

REVERSE BODY LOCK

L is parallel to D in a similar position to the locked half nelson. However, L centers his lock and control on D's lower chest area. L's right arm hooks under D's body and locks with a left arm to the left side of D's body. L's left arm binds D's left arm. L squeezes his elbows tight on D's body, arches his hips down and into D's head and keeps his head and shoulders high (fig. 1).

Figure 1

Figure 2

A variation of the reverse body lock is shown in the photo above. L walks his hips from D's head and goes hip-to-hip with D. L takes an overhook lock on D's left leg and pulls it into his chest. L drives his right leg under D's buttocks to elevate D more onto his shoulder. L's right hand locks around D's body and under D's buttocks on L's right inside thigh. L should not be sitting on his own hips on the mat, but should be arching into D as he drives off his left leg to put D on his back.

HIP TIP

Wrestlers can get very good at moving into this pinning hold off the tight waist breakdown. L controls D's left arm and D's hips are on top of L's left thigh and hips. L pushes off his left leg and arches his hips under D to push D onto his back. L's right shin lifts on D's right calf to prevent D from turning to his stomach. Sometimes L can also control D's left arm by securing it with two-on-one wrist ties. L's right arm would come from between D's legs, pulling D's left forearm and hand into his own crotch area.

REVERSE LEG AND ARM

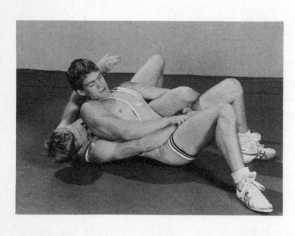

This position is often called a "Peterson." You can finish here after working a lot of rolls, counters and takedown attacks. L controls D's right wrist with his right hand and D's left leg with his left arm hook. L's left hand also grasps D's wrist to help hold D's leg up. L settles his hips down and away, but avoids dropping his buttocks to the mat. L drives his hands, controlling D's wrist, into his crotch as he pushes his back into D's chest and side.

CRADLES

A cradle is applied any time you encircle your opponent's head and leg together in your locked grasp.

L applies a near-side cradle in the photo above (fig. 1). L's right arm, going over D's head and under his chest, locks with L's left arm going around D's right leg. The hands lock tight under D's chest. As L squeezes his elbows to-gether, he can tighten the hold. L's head pushes aside and his hip weight drives into D. L drives D to his back, lifting D's leg and elbow as he squeezes his grip between and under his own chest (fig. 2).

L can also apply a far-side cradle. L crossfaces D with his right arm and secures that hand on D's left elbow (fig. 3). As L drives D's head back around toward his legs, L plants behind D's left thigh. The two hands drive together before L posts his right knee into L's lower back (p. 150, fig. 4). L settles to his right shoulder and hip, pull-

Figure 1

Figure 2

Figure 3

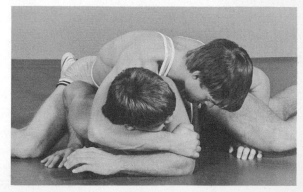

Figure 4

Figure 5

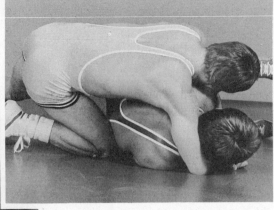

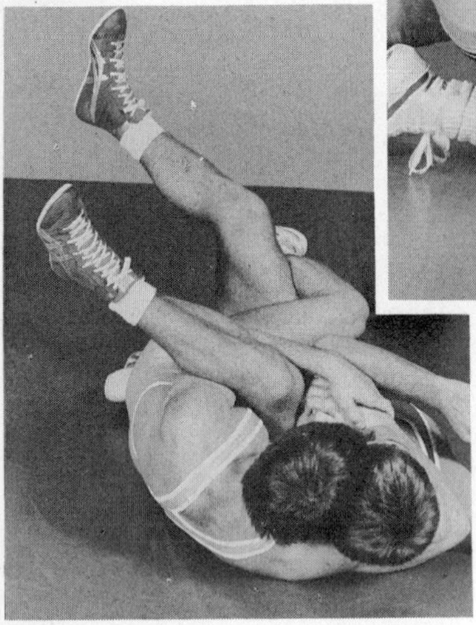

ing D's knee up toward his chest to help bring D's left shoulder to the mat (fig. 5). L also moves his left leg over D's right thigh, clamps his arms tightly together and arches his hips into D.

LEG HOLDS

Often you can use the different leg-ride positions demonstrated in the last chapter in combination with other pinning holds.

In this series of photos (figs. 1, 2 and 3), L uses a facelift, arm bar and elbow lift, respectively, with a leg lace ride. You could use these same holds and others with the leg hook and the leg figure-four as well.

Figure 1

Figure 2

Figure 3

Wrestlers who really want to add variety to their pinning holds will also learn to apply the arm and head holds to the opposite side of their leg rides. In the photo at left (fig. 1), L works a facelift to D's right side with a leg hook applied to D's left side. L can also secure both legs as he turns D on his back. L applies a leg lace with his right leg and a leg hook with his left leg as he works an upper-body hold for the fall on D (fig. 2).

You should also learn to attack your opponent's head and shoulders with the leg combinations. In the photo bottom left (fig. 3), L applies a leg figure-four to D's right arm. L must keep his head and shoulders high and walk his hips counterclockwise, rotating his left knee over D's head to hold him on his back.

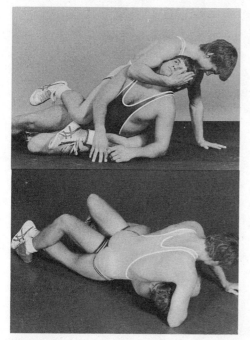

Figure 2

Figure 3

These twelve holds offer positions in which you can secure the fall. Move from your takedowns, counters, rides and breakdowns into the pinning holds. Make them work for you.

Figure 1

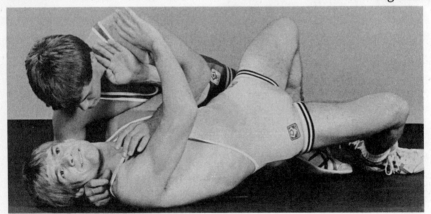

Figure 2

If you get put on your back, you need to use your skills to get off. In the photo above (fig. 1), D uses a head bridge to keep from getting pinned. D drives off his feet and uses a hip arch. In the next photo (fig. 2), L brings his elbow in under D to regain some power to help clear D off him. As L starts to turn off his back, he must use the hip-heist twisting of his hips to get his stomach turned back to the mat and avoid the pin.

Make going for the fall an integral part of your wrestling technique development. The pin is exciting. Go for it!

Chapter 11

THE HUMAN COMPONENTS

There's more—much more—to being the best than simple desire.

Wrestling is one of the most demanding activities in the world. An individual can attain his true potential on the wrestling mat only if he has developed and uses all of the mental, physical and technical tools at his disposal.

TECHNICAL SKILLS

The concern here is with the extent of your wrestling knowledge and its practical use on the mat. This book emphasizes this area the most.

You do not have the opportunity to think about every more you wish to execute during competition. These maneuvers must be instinctive, an automatic reaction to the position and movement of your opponent. By repeatedly going through your movements in drilling sessions you will become familiar with particular reactions and be able to function reflexively in actual matches.

Live wrestling in the practice room allows you to test your technique and gives you an accurate idea of the intensity needed to make the maneuvers work. Of course, live wrestling also involves actual wrestling competition. Though you may wrestle full speed in both practice and meets, the quality of your performance may vary greatly. The psychological impact of structured competition requires getting accustomed to wrestling in meets as much as you can.

PSYCHOLOGICAL PREPARATION

If you want something badly enough and are willing to work hard in quest of it, you probably will attain it. Be sure to set goals for yourself that are realistic, but at the same time ones that will challenge your potential. Don't compare yourself to anyone; your best and someone else's best may be worlds apart. Know where you are going and work hard to get there. If the goals you establish are truly meaningful to you then you must be willing to discipline yourself to do whatever is necessary to accomplish them. Success comes to those who, during their training and development, did things they didn't really want to do or didn't really have to do. Commitment and sacrifice pay dividends.

Just as you can train the body you can train the mind. You have to win the mental victories first. A good book on the subject is *Sports Psyching* by Thomas Tutko and Umberto Tosi, from Jeremy P. Tarcher, Inc.

WEIGHT CONTROL AND NUTRITION

It is important to keep in mind that nutrition is a vital factor in developing your technical, mental and physiological tools. Nothing will diminish the other areas more dramatically than poor nutrition. Two good books on the subject are *Food for Sport* by Dr. Nathan J. Smith, Bell Publishing, and *Eat to Win*, by Robert Haas, Rawson Associates.

Weight cutting is unfortunately a very real problem in the sport of wrestling. For many it has involved dehydration or starvation or both. For a growing boy this can be disastrous. Your body is approximately three-fourths water and the loss of a small percentage of this water can affect your performance and health. You need a nutritious, balanced diet for your body to develop properly.

Water loss through the use of rubber suits, saunas and so forth should not be encouraged. It is recommended that all athletes have fat fold tests to determine body fat percentage before starting to work out or cut weight.

Losing weight is very simple to understand, but that doesn't mean it's easy to do. Weight loss revolves around one thing: calorie intake versus calorie expenditure. Food is burned in the body much like wood in a hot stove. Just as energy released from fuels is used to heat homes and power machinery, the energy released from foods heats our bodies and drives our human machinery. The total energy requirement of an individual is dependent on the amount of energy required for maintaining bodily functions and physical activity. In other words, food intake in calories must be less than the calories being burned if one is to lose weight. And because the body is at a calorie deficit when losing weight we must take in nutritious calories if we are to have optimal body function.

Many people think that in order to lose weight you must eat only protein. This is not true.

The optimum diet for health would break down like this:

	Fat	*Protein*	*Carbohydrates*
Optimum Diet for Health	30–35%	12–15%	55–58%
Average American Diet	43%	12%	45%

One pound of fat equals 3,500 calories, so to lose one pound of fat a person must burn 3,500 more calories than he takes in. Three basic methods are used to burn calories:

- *Basal metabolism,* which is the energy expended for breathing and organ functions and equals approximately 1,400 calories.
- *Daily activities,* which involves school, work, walking and so forth, and varying with the amount or activity in a given day, usually equals about 800 calories.
- *Practice and added workouts,* which would have the greatest influence on calorie loss. One hour of wrestling practice would equal approximately 1,000–1,200 calories.

Combining these activities, we find an expenditure of about 3,400 calories per day, meaning one would lose a pound a day if one did not eat at all. This is not much, but the key to losing weight is to do things slowly and lose two to three pounds per week. This way one can maintain optimal body function by maintaining good nutrition in the diet.

The keys to controlling weight are time and discipline.

PHYSIOLOGICAL DEVELOPMENT

It is important to understand the physical demands that wrestling puts on the body. Once you do, you can train to improve your physiological state and consequently your performance level. Understand your body and its needs. There is no good excuse for a poorly conditioned body.

Physiologically, you need muscular fitness, flexibility and cardio-respiratory fitness to better assure success on the wrestling mat.

Muscular fitness refers to muscle strength and muscle endurance, or your ability to repeatedly perform a task. Muscular fitness can be achieved through a combination of wrestling and a host of auxiliary programs, including running and a weight-training program.

Flexibility is vital to wrestling because of the twisting, turning, straining nature of the sport. A flexible joint in the body allows powerful action through the entire range of motion of that particular joint.

A conscientious, sound weight-training program will also promote flexibility. Flexibility exercise should precede wrestling practice sessions to prepare the muscle and joints for intense activity. A flexible person stands less chance of injury and is more capable of performing a variety of movements.

Your program of flexibility should work the back, hips, shoulders, elbows, wrists, neck, knees and ankles.

Cardio-respiratory fitness involves the efficiency of the heart and lung system in getting fuel and oxygen to the working muscle, and removing carbon dioxide and other waste products. The heart, just like any other muscle, works better if it is stronger. A training program that promotes the improved capacity of the heart-lung system will allow you to work harder, longer.

In general, to get a training effect on the heart you must perform activities that stress the heart for extended periods of time (about twelve to fifteen minutes of work with the heart rate between 130 and 150 beats per minute). A hard two-mile run stresses the heart sufficiently to get a training effect. Other beneficial activities include wrestling, cycling, jumping rope and a properly used weight-training program.

CONDITIONING OFF THE MAT

Wrestling is its own best conditioner. The problem is that it's hard to just wrestle all the time and not lose a little enthusiasm in your preparation. Change-of-pace activities can relieve the doldrums and augment your ability to get in shape for wrestling.

We've got to be concerned with increasing our aerobic capacity, much as a distance runner must, but not to the same degree. Also we must improve our anaerobic power (this involves short-term bursts of energy, like a sprinter's).

What things can help us here?

- Jumping rope, which is great for balance, timing and conditioning.
- Riding a bike (many of the new stationary ones are great).
- Lifeline Gyms, rowing ergometers, cross-country ski machines and Universal Real Runners are other excellent supplements to your conditioning workout.
- Running. Don't just jog. Good wrestlers run a lot, sometimes every day. Sprint work is good early in the week before a competition and on alternate days.

A long-distance run with periodic sprints—100s and 220s—inserted is an ideal workout because it mirrors an actual wrestling match. Run stadium steps, bleachers or steep hills. I think a good wrestler must get in a minimum of twelve miles a week in running training.

Here are some interesting and effective running sequences used in wrestling training:

Walk-Jog-Sprint: This workout was first introduced to me when I was a member of the U.S. World and Pan-American Games teams in

1975. A course was marked off every eighty to hundred yards. The idea was to walk to the first marker, jog to the next, and sprint hard to the third before repeating the sequence. It seemed easy at first, but after forty-five minutes . . .

Catches: Put three people in a group on a 220-yard track. Two of the three sprint off around the track while the third jogs in place until the sprinters complete the circuit. One of the sprinters then becomes a jogger while the other two sprint another circuit. On the next lap, the third man takes his turn jogging while his partners finish the sprint.

Increase the total number of catches as conditioning improves. You can also increase or decrease the number in a group.

Indian Run: Set up a group of six to eight wrestlers jogging in tandem around a track; they should be a couple of steps apart. Running at a medium jogging pace (depending on conditioning level), the last man in a tandem moves to the outside of the line and sprints to the front. As he reaches the head of the line, the man to the rear sprints to the front. This continues for however many laps have been designated. It will get to be very demanding if the overall pace is good. Try to keep wrestlers of comparable ability in each group. Slow athletes will break up the flow of the run.

Walk the Curves, Sprint the Straightaways: Put a small group of athletes together and have them either walk or jog the ends of the track and all sprint a measured distance down the sides. These can become very competitive and are a tremendous conditioner. Increase the number of total laps as the athletes get in better shape.

Buddy Carries: Establish a prescribed distance and have the wrestlers pair up. Each athlete carries his partner piggyback for a couple of hundred steps, switching off until the total distance is covered. Watch the bad ankles, knees and backs on this. Try it up steep terrain as well.

The great thing about running is that your imagination can make every practice different and challenging. Beat the ho-hum of three times around the block.

WEIGHT TRAINING

Year-round strength training should represent a major portion of a wrestler's preparation. Unfortunately, many athletes and their coaches ignore this much-needed facet of preparation, the assumption often being that all a wrestler needs to do is wrestle. While there is no one way to train, there are certain truths regarding the body and how it adapts to applied stress.

WHY STRENGTH TRAIN

In recent years no other single development has made as great an impact on the world of sport as strength training. All other things being equal, the stronger athlete will enjoy greater success, avoid injury more easily, recover from injury sooner and perform the movements of his sport with greater ease and efficiency.

In no sport are these statements more true than in wrestling, one of the most demanding sports on earth. A wrestler is constantly called upon to exhibit total body strength and power, which can only be fully realized through year-round strength training.

A properly implemented strength program will:

- Improve muscular endurance.
- Improve the measure of power demonstrated by an athlete. Power, the union of strength and speed, is crucial to a wrestler's success. The ability to perform explosively is necessary to success.
- Enhance joint and muscle flexibility.
- Enhance full-range strength and power.
- Increase lean body mass.
- Increase or enhance neuromuscular efficiency, the ability to call on or "recruit" muscle fibers by the central nervous system or brain.
- Improve heart-lung performance. Although the debate on aerobic benefits resulting from strength training is still going on, there are gains to be made, the most noticeable being the increase in the number of capillaries and the improvement of cardiac efficiency.

- Alter basal metabolic rate. Basal metabolism is the minimum metabolic activity required to maintain such life processes as heartbeat and respiration. Weight training can alter one's basal metabolism so calories ingested are used efficiently.

When developing a strength program, keep the following fundamentals in mind to realize maximum gains and train in a safe, efficient manner.

Technique: Whether you are just starting a weight training program or trying to improve the one you have, it is crucial that you emphasize proper technique. As in wrestling, proper technique in lifting is the difference between great and poor results. Poor technique can, and often does, result in injury that could have been avoided.

Range of Movement: Due to the nature of wrestling, the range of movement used while lifting is a major consideration. Contrary to myths associated with weight training, flexibility can be enhanced through the use of resistance training. The musculature that surrounds each joint determines the flexibility of that joint. If through the use of stretching or full range of movement exercise the joint is required to go through its full range of motion, it will retain its natural elasticity. The problem of limited flexibility is the result of limited or abbreviated movement. A muscle will tend to tighten when it is not forced to move through its full range.

Full range movement will result in full range strength. The use of maximum strength through a muscle's full range of movement is crucial to a wrestler or other athlete.

Speed of Movement: During exercise, constant, even resistance must be employed against a muscle through its whole range of motion. If a high, momentum-producing speed is used while lifting, force is only fully supplied at the beginning and end of the movement. Momentum carries some percentage of the weight during the middle of the lift, allowing the muscle to rest.

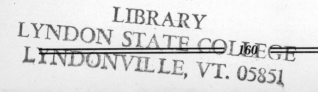